EVERYDAY ANTIQUES

JJ DESPAIN

STOREY
BOOKS

The mission of Storey Communications is to serve our customers
by publishing practical information that encourages personal independence
in harmony with the environment.

Edited by Deborah Balmuth and Marie Salter
Copyedited by Laura Jorstad
Cover design by Beth Carlisle
Cover and interior photographs by Giles Prett
Illustrations by Rick Daskam
Photostyling on pages 165–167, 168 (bottom), 169–174, 175 (bottom), and 176–179 by Robin
    Brickman; photographs on pages 168 (top), 175 (top), and 180 produced by Bruce Shostak
Text design and production by Susan Bernier
Production assistance by Jennifer Jepson Smith
Indexed by Susan Olason / Indexes & Knowledge Maps

Printed in Canada by Transcontinental Printing
10 9 8 7 6 5 4 3 2 1

Library of Congress Cataloging-in-Publication Data

Despain, JJ
    Everyday Antiques / JJ Despain.
        p. cm.
    Includes index.
    ISBN 1-58017-249-0 (alk. paper)
    1. House furnishings. 2. Secondhand trade—United States. 3. Collectibles in interior decoration. 4. Antiques in interior decoration. I. Title.
    TX315 .D47 2000
    645—dc21

00-026549

DEDICATION

This book is dedicated to my mother,
Marguerite Holmes, and my grandmother,
Nana White, who both taught me to cherish the old;
and to my husband, Joel, my truest supporter
in both writing and antiques hunting.

ACKNOWLEDGMENTS

Pat Irwin, a trusted and literate friend who cleans up the typos.

Brent Holmes, an antiques expert in his own right.

The Allisonville Road Antiques mall in Indianapolis, Indiana: thanks for letting me photograph your place.

The experts of the *Antique Bottle & Glass Collector*, who enlighten me every month.

The publishers of *Collectors News & the Antique Trader*, who gave me the opportunity to write about what I know.

Nasty, Stinky, and all the good ol' boys who have taught me well.

And finally, Joyce Layton, a friend in antiquing whom I miss, but whose knowledge and wisdom live on in those who knew her.

Storey Books extends a special thank you to Robin Brickman and Jeff Strait, Caroline Burch, Jenny Cummings, Debbie Elder and Collector's Warehouse, Pauline Guntlow, Nancy Lamb, Meredith Maker, Cindy McFarland, Martien and Cynthia Mulder, and Gwen and Dick Steege, for allowing us to photograph their "everyday antiques."

Introduction

Welcome to the wonderful world of antiques and collectibles! If you haven't yet opened the door to take a peek at all those treasures that could be yours, now's a great time to do it: Antiquing is quickly becoming one of the most popular pastimes in the United States. If you have opened that door but you'd like a little more insight into what you can do with those treasures once you've found them, or how and where you can make better deals, you've come to the right place. I'm an avid collector, an antiques writer, a sometime picker (one who buys antiques for others), and an all-around enthusiast for the lifestyle. And going on the hunt *does* become a lifestyle. So perhaps I can unravel some of those not-so-deep mysteries for you and offer a little information that will help you become a more knowledgeable shopper.

MODEST BEGINNINGS

My first antique came to me when I married my husband. Into our marriage he brought his clothes, an alarm clock, a pair of scissors, a few books, and an old whiskey bottle he'd dug up in the Utah desert when he was a kid.

I'd have preferred a new Ferrari and a cabin on the lake, but his most treasured possession was that old bottle with the name QUAKER MAID WHISKEY on it. Its bottom was filled with three inches of hard clay, it was scratched and not very pretty, and it was clear glass instead of a beautiful antique color. All in all, there was really little appeal for me in this piece of junk, but it held a sentimental value for my husband because of the way in which he'd found it. So begrudgingly I cleaned out the clay, washed the bottle, and set it on a shelf for display. And there it sat for a year — something to be dusted, something that was always in the way, something that took up good space.

SERENDIPITY

The bottle looked lonely. I'm one for symmetry in decoration, and I had absolutely nothing that would make a symmetrical display with that old thing, so it sat alone. Then one day, on a whim, I went to a country flea market — my first ever. As I wandered around, perplexed by all the different and strange things people were buying, I discovered a large cardboard box filled with other old bottles. A few didn't look too bad, and I envisioned them as companions to my husband's bottle. In my mind I saw a nice symmetrical display, and I'll admit what I envisioned didn't look too bad. Since the whole box cost only a dollar, I lugged it home and set out a few mates for the Quaker Maid.

CURIOSITY

After weeks of dusting the new trinkets along with the original one, I began to wonder what they were. My husband's bottle was clearly marked as a whiskey bottle, so

These old bottles, c. 1880–1890, were practical containers for medicine and whiskey (Quaker Maid), and it's a sure bet the people who bought them with their original contents didn't pay more than a dollar or two. Wouldn't they be surprised to find that more than one hundred years later those same bottles, empty, would sell from $10 to $50? Vintage and antique bottles are among the top collectibles, and their prices reflect their popularity.

the only mystery there was the bottle's age. So I searched the library for a book on antique bottles. Much to my delight, I learned that the Quaker Maid bottle was about 120 years old. The value wasn't much, somewhere around $30 at the time, but the age of the thing really excited me, especially since I'd been reluctant to allow this venerable piece of glass a few inches of shelf space in my home. An authentic Wild West whiskey bottle found buried in the sand — can you imagine the images that conjured up? It was exciting to attach a provenance to my husband's bottle, even if it was a fantasy. Pretty soon that piece of junk became a real piece of western Americana in my description of it to friends.

When I researched the other bottles I'd purchased, I learned that one was closer to 150 years old and had been used in food storage. Three others were about 120 years old and had contained medicine — that old patent medicine that became popular in the late nineteenth century. That was an exciting discovery, too, even though much later I learned that in the bottle world, my purchases were pretty common and not very valuable. Still, carting home a box of genuine antiques for a buck was a new experience for me, and I'll have to admit that all those bottles sitting alongside my husband's find did take on an intriguing quality.

PROVENANCE
An object's history. Verifiable provenance enhances value.

A PROUD, GROWING COLLECTION

Today those few bottles are joined by dozens of others in all colors and shapes. I rotate our bottles with the seasons and for different household decorations. I use bathroom bottles to decorate my bathrooms, and food and kitchen bottles to adorn my kitchen. And I change my displays with the hundreds, maybe even thousands, of other bottles stored in boxes in my garage, all worthy of display and begging to be set out for a while. What's more, I love to drag out those boxes and just look at our collection — all of which is, in a sense, the offspring of a single old bottle dug out of the desert sand.

Some of our bottles have value; others sell for only a few dollars. My most recent ventures have been in search of old food bottles with intact paper labels. Original paper labels belonging on the bottle to which they are attached are hard to find and difficult to maintain, so this is an area of collecting my husband and I have never tackled before. I'll admit that I won't pay more than about $15 for a bottle, which makes me pretty cheap, but because of my years of hunting other treasures I know there are some great paper-label bottles out there at the price I'm willing to pay. The only thing is, my set price makes the hunt a little more difficult. But then, hunting is most of the fun for me, even though I do take immense pleasure in the owning, too. And while our bottle collection has certainly grown in value and quality far beyond a single Quaker Maid Whiskey bottle with a lump of clay in the bottom, I still love looking for a great deal on a cheap paper-label bottle, or something to put in my bathroom, or something I'm not even aware that I'm looking for until I see it.

THE APPEAL OF EVERYDAY ANTIQUES

Why do I enjoy the thrill of the hunt so much? Because I've discovered the joy of decorating my home with the antiques and collectibles I buy. And these aren't the kind of antiques and collectibles you rope off so no one can sit on them. They're the ones I use every day — the 1930s kitchen utensils, the early-1900s electric lighting, the mid-1800s oil lamps, the circa-1680 German immigrant trunk, the circa-1850 handmade wooden chair, and the circa-1820 solid cherry dresser.

My favorite yellow mixing bowl is part of a popular 1940s set given to many young brides back then. The whole set was a gift to my mother, from her mother, on her wedding day in 1947. Years later, when my grandmother came to live with us, she taught me to cook using those bowls. We mixed sugar cookies in them, and pie filling and bread dough. Eventually three bowls out of the set were broken, but after the lone yellow bowl was handed down to me, I was able to replace the others for just a few dollars, making the set complete again. Now, even though my mother and grandmother are gone, both are still with me in spirit when I pull out the old yellow bowl. It really doesn't matter that the other bowls are replacements; the memories that come with them are genuine. And for me, recapturing memories is a big part of why I love shopping for antiques and collectibles.

THEY DON'T MAKE THINGS LIKE THEY USED TO ...

When I shop for my home today, my first thought is something old. I once needed a new spice set, so I went to an antiques mall to find one that had been popular in the 1930s. I found some great old table linens, too, and their fifty years' worth of wear give them an appearance more interesting than new ones. And I mix and match. Who says my fifty-year-old table runner can't go on my two-hundred-year-old table? Or that the table my great-grandfather made in 1870 can't hold a 1940s lamp?

Even though this bowl isn't very old, just over fifty years, it has a history of being part of the sugar cookies, bread, and melt-in-your-mouth yeast rolls Nana White made for her family. And they were the best! Bowls like this are common in most antiques and collectibles venues, but the mouth-watering treats you mix in them are best made from your own family recipes.

When it comes to antiques and collectibles, no rules dictate what you should like and how you should use what you buy for your home. If you want to rope off an old chair for display purposes only, that's fine. If you want to sit on it, that's fine, too. As you read *Everyday Antiques,* you'll learn that many household antiques and collectibles had practical uses when they were invented that are just as practical today. And one of the greatest discoveries you might make is that what was created years ago, in many cases, is of better quality than what is created today. That's why my kitchen utensil drawer is full of everything but new utensils. My old spoons are sturdier than anything you can buy brand new today, and you'd have to beat me over the head with my grandmother's wooden rolling pin to get it away from me, because its glide across pie pastry is so much smoother and more experienced than what I got with the new rolling pin I purchased shortly after I was married.

ENJOY YOUR TREASURES!

Antiques and collectibles are meant to be enjoyed, either on display or in use. As you read these pages and learn how to do many of the things I've done with my treasures, my wish is that you'll find the same enjoyment in your antiques and collectibles that I've already found, and will continue to find, in mine.

Who, What, When, Where, and Why

C ontrary to what many people think, *antiquing* or shopping for collectibles is not just a pastime for avid collectors and professionals anymore. Everyone does it. Young couples are setting up housekeeping with bedroom suites, dining room sets, knickknacks, and all sorts of housewares purchased from antiques malls and flea markets. People who have chipped a plate or are missing a cup and saucer from their favorite everyday dishes are out there looking for replacements instead of discarding the rest or being reduced to a seven-place setting. Good friends are buying that perfect *something old* or *something blue* bridal gift. Nostalgia hunters are looking for a trace of their past in a replica of the toy they played with until it wore out or the candy dish identical to the one on Grandma's coffee table — the one she always kept filled with those delicious pink mints.

The good news is that because of the popularity of hunting for reminders of the past, replacements, special gifts, and everyday items, more antiques and collectibles are available now than ever before. They're coming out of closets and down from attics. Boxes of them are being carted up from basements and dragged out of garages.

Old barns are being raided and storage sheds emptied, simply because people are discovering how appealing the old and venerable pieces really are. And yes, people are incorporating their treasures into their home decor, enjoying the aesthetic beauty of some items while putting others to practical use.

The even-better news? Because antiques and collectibles are for sale in such abundance and at such good prices, it's a shopper's market.

Who Are the Shoppers?

The shoppers are your mother, your next-door neighbor, and your best friend. Ministers are shopping. So are truck drivers. Farmers are out there on the hunt, along with schoolteachers and professional athletes. In other words, shoppers cross every economic, racial, and professional boundary. Let's take a look at a few of the shoppers you will encounter on your own shopping expeditions.

Antiques and Collectibles Experts

The world of antiques and collectibles is filled with experts. Generally, they're people who know a little about many different items — or a considerable amount about one or two specific things, such as Civil War memorabilia or oil lamps. Experts write books and magazine articles; they appraise, collect, and restore; and as often as not they also deal in antiques and collectibles. If you've been to a flea market lately, you've probably seen dealers who specialize only in die-cast cars, for instance, or old magazines and other forms of paper advertising. These are people who have, most likely, become experts out of their own interest in a particular area. In antiques and collectibles, interest almost always builds knowledge.

EPHEMERA
Paper collectibles, including old magazines and all forms of paper advertising.

Learn from the Experts

Be observant when you shop. Experts are shopping right beside you; watch what they do and listen to the questions they ask. They usually stick out in an antiques crowd, so if you think you've spotted one, be bold and ask a few questions. Experts love to share their knowledge. And in the long run, what an expert knows can help you along your own road to gaining expertise. Here are some questions to ask of an expert:

- What's the age of the item?
- How can you tell if it's authentic?
- What's it worth in mint condition?
- What's it worth in *this* condition?

Warning! Even though you've cornered a wonderful expert who's willing to answer all your questions, be a little wary. Many simply aren't what they claim to be. If the story you hear sounds too elaborate, or if something about it doesn't seem to fit, counter with specific questions such as:

- How do you know that?
- Can that fact be verified?
- Where can I find a good resource that will tell me more?

A real expert can answer these questions readily.

In today's world of antiques and collectibles, there are general experts, and then there are the real experts. A general expert has some knowledge, often from books or the hands-on experience that comes from dealing with certain kinds of antiques. This is the kind of expert you'll most commonly encounter. He'll look at an old bottle and tell you it's an antique, probably used on a dresser or mantel, and he'll quote a price based on a similar bottle he saw for sale in another show or mall.

The real expert, however, has gone beyond a basic familiarity with old bottles to seek out more knowledge, whether from university studies in antiquities or history, or through personal associations with others in the field. He will verify that the old bottle was, indeed, used on a

This Harden Fire Grenade is typical of most fire grenades predating 1900. Usually filled with water or salt water, it was lobbed onto the fire when needed, so that the glass shattered and released its contents. In the earliest American fire departments, firefighters would carry huge bottles, called carboys, containing several gallons of water to a fire and throw them in. Any fire grenade is a lovely knickknack for setting on a shelf, and these grenades have particular appeal to those who collect or are interested in fire-fighting mementos.

dresser or mantel, and its original content — usually water — was meant to put out fires. He will go on to tell you that the bottle was intended to be lobbed directly into a fire, that it dates to about 1880, that it's called a fire grenade, and that it was manufactured by a company named Harden. Then he will let you know that the early fire grenade is the forerunner of today's fire extinguisher as well as the military hand grenade used in combat. Last, but not least, the real expert will assess the bottle's rarity and give you an accurate appraisal based on the current market value for Harden fire grenades. So as you can see, the general expert does have information based on his experience, but the real expert is someone who specializes in old bottles or fire grenades and has specific information based on his study of the field.

Antiques and Collectibles Dealers

Dealers are shopping next to you, too. In fact, dealers are among the best and most avid shoppers wherever antiques and collectibles are sold because, like everyone else, they are looking for just that perfect item to buy. In their case, however, the item is intended for resale in their own shop or flea market booth.

For the shopper, antiques and collectibles are available in abundant supply, but for the dealer, reasonably priced stock that can be bought and resold for a decent profit is decreasing because people are becoming more savvy in their treasure hunting. Thanks to several popular television shows, the general public is now alerted to the possibility that the junk in their attic could be of value. And you're probably keeping your fingers crossed that the old sword you found in the attic rafters and then played with as a child is an authentic Civil War weapon worth thousands of dollars. Years ago you might have stuck it in a

garage sale knowing only that it was an old sword, and you probably would have been happy with the $50 you received. Now that you've seen the antiques program where a sword resembling yours sold for $30,000, though, you're not about to part with it until you learn more about it — its history and especially its value. Right?

Since you've made that discovery, or become aware that other people are making similar discoveries, you simply aren't as likely to let go of any of your attic junk until you've had everything appraised or have done the appropriate research yourself. This trend of discover-before-you-sell is hurting the dealer who could once depend on buying that attic full of junk for just a few dollars and a promise to dust out the cobwebs and sweep the floors. Consequently, he is out there shopping, too, looking for something priced far enough below market value to buy and resell for a reasonable profit. Believe it or not, this happens all the time. Most dealers with a line of general merchandise don't have the expertise to recognize the true value of everything they are offering, making it very easy for those dealers who *are* experts to find great buys in the shops and booths of their fellow dealers. This is something every dealer knows can, and does, happen. Every dealer's worst nightmare is to sell that old wooden bowl to another dealer for $25, then see it in her shop priced at $600.

As well as the shops of other dealers, garage and rummage sales are extremely popular among those who sell antiques, especially if the sale has been advertised as offering antiques or collectibles. When an announcement has been posted, count on a flock of dealers converging on the sale before anyone else gets there. Frequently, they will contact the seller and ask for a shot

Civil War relics are some of the most popular all-American collectibles today, much because of their colorful history, but also because of their increasing value. This sword and sash were the property of a captain in the Union army and have remained in their original family, being handed down from first son to first son since the 1860s.

Sewing stools were a necessity for the housewife who had mending to do — as most did. It was sturdy enough to serve as a seat, and it was practical because the seat lifted off to reveal a storage area where all the sewing notions could be stored. This c. 1860 model still serves its original function, holding scissors, needles, pins, and buttons.

at early buying; offer to buy everything in the sale before anything is offered to the public; or even go so far as to show up several hours early, parking themselves in the best place to make a mad dash for the garage the instant the door opens.

No matter where you're shopping or browsing, chances are that half the people shoving their way through the crowds to get at the best stuff are dealers looking for a fresh supply of merchandise for their own displays.

Interior Designers

Look in the rafters of your favorite home-cooking restaurant. Do you see an old wagon wheel, typewriter, pair of skates, or sign advertising a cola that hasn't been in existence in your lifetime? The person who purchased these things probably shopped the same flea market you shopped two weeks ago and may be at the next one in which you find yourself browsing.

Interior designers are always on the hunt for specific items to incorporate into a theme — a room of fine old furniture, a dresser that will match an existing bed, or a few older knickknacks to fill up a wall. Many people today want nice antiques and collectibles in their homes or businesses, but they have neither the time nor the expertise

Should You Ever Overbid?

If you know you're competing with a dealer to buy an old sewing stool, and you're desperate to own it, offer more money than what's being asked. Dealers are forced to set limits on what they can afford to spend in order to make a profit, and if you're able to exceed that limit, the stool will likely find a nice place in your home. In other words, do a little overbidding if you really *have* to have it. Just don't offer more than you can afford to pay.

necessary to find what they want, let alone an idea about what will fit into their existing decor. As a result, they rely on a professional to plan the design, make the purchases, and blend everything together so old and new can coexist gracefully. And if you think that an interior designer shops only the finest antiques and collectibles venues while you are perusing the flea markets and rummage sales, think again. Any shopping outlet with vintage merchandise is fair game. That person you saw examining an old granite bucket is just as likely to be looking for something to fill a shelf at a folksy diner as he is to be a collector or dealer looking for something to own or sell.

Professional Shoppers

Yes, you will encounter these people, too. Called *pickers* by those in the antiques and collectibles business, they shop for clients with specific wish lists. Collectors, dealers, and investors are at the top of a picker's client list. Pickers operate in one of two ways: They buy an item and resell it to the client, or they spend the client's money to make the purchase. Either way, it's a great job for people who love the hunt.

Do-It-Yourself Home Decorators

The past decade has brought a new awareness of antiques and collectibles — not just as someone's discards or a pursuit for the very wealthy, but as an accessible, practical, and affordable way to furnish a home. Antiques outlets exist that specialize in furniture from every period in history, the 1960s as well as the 1860s. Each has its own unique look, and you can outfit an entire home from a favorite period.

An interesting phenomenon is that do-it-yourself home decorators have elevated furnishing a home with

VINTAGE
Something made in an earlier time.

An old granite bucket has many more functions than hauling water. It's a great place to stack magazines or newspapers and makes an unique container for fresh or silk flowers. Pine cones, poinsettias, and holly sprigs look beautiful in graniteware at Christmas. But if the need arises, the bucket will still carry water if it hasn't rusted through in a spot or two.

used furniture from a stigma to a goal. Certainly, anyone who has purchased a Victorian love seat for $100 has a right to brag, but it wasn't too long ago that the love seat would have been labeled *used*, not *Victorian*. The term *used* has always connoted objects purchased by people in financial need — college students, young newlyweds, anyone not yet financially solvent enough to buy *new*.

Fortunately, *used* has taken on a different image, and it's not uncommon to find homemakers looking for something used rather than new. In fact, if something used has any kind of a place in the home or place of business, people are hunting for it. Today, even clothing is tagged *vintage* and sold in antiques and collectibles outlets as well as specialty shops handling only vintage clothing. And guess what? It's popular. An electrician went to rewire a bedroom-turned-closet and was amazed by the racks and racks of vintage clothing he found there. Some items were hanging, others were displayed on mannequins, while several things were arranged in an old mercantile display cabinet. A shelf spanning the length of an entire wall held high-top, button-up shoes. And there were hats and scarves, and an ample collection of old purses and undergarments.

Styles change, as you can see from the c. 1860 Victorian chair on the left and the chair on the right, made one hundred years later. Wood, fiberglass, cloth, or chrome — the materials don't matter if the chair fits your decorating scheme. Remember though, that whether the piece originates from 1860 or 1960, original condition is the best.

Added to that mix of shoppers who love the older merchandise for its own sake are environmentally conscious individuals who have always heeded their responsibility to recycle. Once they were the only ones dragging home the living room furniture straight from the 1950s *I Love Lucy* television program, but now they have company and a lot of stiff competition, especially since the *used* tag is now so often replaced by one reading *vintage*. It's amazing the difference a word can make. In this case it has created a shopping frenzy when good antiques and collectibles hit the market, and those who are decorating their homes and buying for other personal reasons are right in the thick of it.

Collectors and Browsers

Where there are antiques and collectibles for sale, there will always be collectors and browsers, and these are the other shoppers with whom you'll be bumping elbows when you go on your own hunt. The nature of a collector is anything from avid to obsessive, and money is not always an object when just the right piece is presented for sale, especially if that piece has been the focus of a long search. One enthusiastic collector found a condiment set she'd been hunting for years, and her screams of excitement brought everyone from nearby aisles in the antiques mall over to see her discovery. As excited as she was by the first set, she was twice as excited when she saw that the dealer had another tucked away, and she whooped and hollered all the way to the cash register, where she paid for the two sets without first asking the price. That price turned out to be about $3,000 per set, and she didn't even blink.

Collectors know exactly what they are looking for, and they will march through an antiques or collectibles outlet with a purpose. Browsers, on the other hand, browse.

Button-up, high-top shoes were the height of fashion just over a century ago, and today they are the height of vintage fashion collectibles. And yes, many women who collect them (sorry guys, but your feet just won't fit) do wear them for special, Victorian dress occasions.

They are looking for any item that strikes their fancy, or sometimes nothing at all. Maybe they're just passing time on a rainy day or wandering through memory lane searching for something that reminds them of their past, their grandmother, or a dear old friend. Browsers meander and enjoy. And occasionally they do buy.

WHAT'S AN ANTIQUE? WHAT'S A COLLECTIBLE?

Some people will say that an *antique* is anything more than twenty or thirty years old. Others will argue that anything 150 years old barely fits the category. Even Noah Webster hedges on his definition by saying an antique is "of ancient times, old, out-of-date or the style of a former period."

Webster's definition notwithstanding, most experts in the United States generally concede the century mark: If it's one hundred years old, it's an antique. So does that mean something eighty or ninety years old isn't an antique? For the purposes of this book, yes. Pieces of advanced age can be called vintage or period pieces, but the line of definition has to be drawn somewhere, and the hundred-year marker is as good a place as any. Now, don't get all upset because your grandmother's precious 1920s birdcage has been demoted to something other than an antique. *Antique* is a relative term — relative to age, not value. That birdcage may fall a few years short of the official *antique* label, but that in no way diminishes its value.

Since we've established an antique as something that's a hundred years old or older, what is a collectible? Quite simply, a *collectible* is anything you deem worth

In 1920 this birdcage was likely the home of a pair of lovebirds or a canary with a beautiful song. Today, it's a wonderful decoration all by itself or with a gracefully draping Boston fern inside. And it still makes a great home for a bird, too.

keeping. Most antiques are collectible, but it may surprise you to know that's not the case with all of them. Age doesn't necessarily mean something is worth keeping. For example, a seventy-five-year-old butter churn may well be worth considering a collectible, but is an old piece of rope? Actually, the answer could be yes, if you happen to collect old rope. If old rope is only old rope to you, though, and new rope has more appeal or use in your life, that old rope isn't collectible, at least not to you. The word *collectible,* like the word *antique,* is relative — relative to what you, and only you, think is worth collecting or keeping.

WHEN ARE WE SHOPPING?

Antiques and collectibles are being discovered and purchased every day of the week. Given the new fervor in shopping, the market has become extremely customer friendly, accommodating almost every schedule. Dealers have seen the need to be available when the public wants them to be and, as a result, avid shoppers have grown used to finding an antiques or collectibles outlet open almost anytime they get the urge to shop.

Weekends are the busiest days for most places selling antiques and collectibles, however. In most circumstances, flea markets and antiques flea markets set up for business on Friday and operate through Sunday. Normal operating hours can start as early as 6 A.M. and run well into the evening, especially during the longer days of summer. Finer antiques shows also operate on a three-day weekend, Friday through Sunday, but you may find their opening hours closer to midmorning and their closing hours late into the evening.

Traveling Shows

Antiques shows and flea markets generally appear on a regular, predictable basis. Some are organized to operate every month; others open their doors two or three times a year. In both cases, the schedules are fairly consistent. If your favorite show appeared in March and September this year, chances are it will return at the same times next year.

Seasonal Shows

A great time to find the best selection of merchandise in antiques and collectibles shows is near the Christmas season, from mid-October through the first part of December. If you're lucky, you might be able to keep yourself busy every weekend for weeks as holiday decorations are added to the normal antiques stock. Christmas is, indeed, a time when shoppers become nostalgic for the ornament that always sat atop their childhood tree, or

The Early Bird

Antiques shows post their hours for the general public, but they often make an exception when it comes to early buying hours. For a price, many shows will allow shoppers to browse and make purchases prior to the official opening. The cost for the privilege can be substantial, anywhere from several dollars to $40 or $50, but the big advantages for those interested in serious shopping are the unique opportunities to get a first look at the goods and to make purchases before the general public does. When you attend a show the instant its doors open on the first day and find items already tagged *sold*, you've been beaten by an early buyer. Dealers are usually the ones clamoring to beat the rush, but the opportunity is often open to the general public, too. If you'd like to be one of the early shoppers, contact the managers of the show and ask how to go about it. You can locate managers by calling the facility in which the show is taking place and asking for the information.

find themselves stuck with gift-buying problems and realize that something old can be so much better than something new. Dealers know this, so they gear up for the season. You'll often find Christmas shows not only stocked with more goodies than any other shows of the year but also brimming with more dealers.

Christmas aside, however, dealers also put on a nice display for other holidays, such as Easter and Halloween, when home decorations are traditional and popular. In the past few years, one of the hottest trends in collecting has been holiday decorations, with vintage jack-o'-lanterns and witches running a close second to Santa and his elves. Items commemorating Jewish holidays are highly collectible, too, but are not as abundant, so opportunities to find these are at a premium.

Speaking of holidays, if you're bored by noontime on New Year's Day, go find an antiques mall. Antiques shopping has become a holiday tradition known only to those who have done it before. Many malls are open for holidays, with Christmas being the exception. So when you've had enough of the Fourth of July picnic, or if the Easter bunny bypassed your house altogether, try an antiques mall. You'll be surprised how many other people will be there with you. In fact, you'll be surprised how many people frequent the antiques malls every weekend. Sure, the malls are open during the week, but Saturday and Sunday see the majority of browsers and die-hard shoppers. Many larger malls adjust their normal business hours accordingly, to include a few extra hours on the weekends.

Independent Shops

Shops owned and operated by one person, offering merchandise only from that person, are called *independent shops*. They have a different operating schedule than other

Yes, Virginia, Christmas trees did have lights before electricity. These Victorian Christmas lights, also called float lamps, dating from the 1880s were filled with oil, lit, and hung on the tree. They looked beautiful set among the green pine boughs, flickering red, cobalt blue, teal, white, peacock blue, and purple.

channels through which antiques and collectibles are sold, and it's not uncommon to find that one is actually shut on a weekend. You will almost always find them closed for the holidays. Many small shops are at a disadvantage today because they cannot stock merchandise at prices or in quantities comparable to those you can find in a mall, show, or flea market. Some shop owners actually participate in the weekend enterprises to keep themselves in business. If an independent shop does stay open for the busy time, don't be surprised to find it closed two or three days during the week. Even antiques and collectibles dealers need their rest.

Other Hunting Times

Don't forget garage, yard, and basement sales when you're on the hunt. A few may operate during the week, but the majority of these are weekend ventures, too.

One other thing: Maybe you're a confirmed night owl, and the thought of hunting your treasures during the day is about as appealing as a steady diet of Brussels sprouts and sardines. There's a popular new way for you to shop, and all it takes is access to an Internet server. Yes, the computer age has meandered into the world of antiques and collectibles, and if you can't get to the goods or you simply decide that armchair shopping is more your style, any antique or collectible imaginable is available with a few clicks of a computer key. (See chapter 2 for more about e-shopping.) Don't despair if your hours don't correspond to those of your favorite outlet — you can have a world of antiques and collectibles at your fingertips any time you want.

Shopping by Appointment

Small dealers occasionally open during off-hours by special appointment. This is not a service for the common browser, but if you know that what you can't live without is in a particular shop and that shop's hours don't suit your schedule, call and ask to arrange an appointment. Most dealers will be happy to oblige a serious shopper, even at the most unusual hours.

WHERE ARE WE SHOPPING?

Quick! Think fast. Where do the best American antiques come from? Are you thinking the East? Most people do because traditionally, the best antiques *were* found on the East Coast. Since America's eastern half was settled before its western, many of the pieces that came to this country with early immigrants, or that were made here by new settlers, stayed east even when society moved west. They were simply too cumbersome to move overland and across the mountains, and early pioneers lacked the means and ability to transport anything more than food, clothing, some livestock, and family. Hence, the pieces that found their home on the East Coast, or were left behind, became desirable to collectors because they were known to be the oldest in the United States. And for most antiques hunters, older is always best.

Another interesting aspect of early East Coast antiques is that the wood from that geographic area, used in furniture making, was generally harder and featured a prettier grain than wood found in the western half of the country. This made eastern furniture more desirable and added to the illusion that East Coast antiques were better. The truth is that it was all a matter of awareness and appreciation. As the nineteenth century rolled into the twentieth, the wood found in the western states — primarily pine — was pressed into service and given due recognition for its own brand of beauty and usefulness. This newfound recognition brought a more respectable image to all western antiques and collectibles.

Years ago a quaint little shop or elegant gallery located someplace in the eastern United States was the height of antiques and collectibles shopping, but in the early twentieth century that trend began to change. Thanks to cowboys, Indians, and those legendary Wild West heroes, an unique group of collectibles became popular. After that came an awakening interest in regional favorites, such as pottery, baskets, and other relics associated with Native American culture and slave relics from the South. Antiques dealers began to expand by seeking out regional collectibles and incorporating them into their traditional East Coast collections. Pretty soon the people who were once convinced that East was best began to embrace what the West had to offer, wanting more.

Today there is a huge market for western collectibles, but the supply is scarce because the West was settled a relatively short time ago compared to the East. Also, manufacturers in the Old West simply didn't have the time span in which to create an abundant supply of anything considered collectible today.

The true American antiques market — one that wasn't mixed and mingled with European antiques — began to boom after the United States reached its 150th anniversary, and everything made here, when the country was brand new, suddenly began to look good to collectors. The amazing thing is that what is antique by American standards is often considered just old in other countries around the world. And other cultures literally laugh at our lust for American pieces that might be only one or two hundred years old; they're dealing with similar items several hundred years older. But because the United States is a new country, so are its native antiques.

As antiquing began to branch out and span the entire country, so did the traditional means by which dealers sold antiques and collectibles. Secondhand shops became a venue, if the hunters knew what they were looking for.

So did flea markets. Eventually, flea markets selling only antiques and collectibles came onto the scene, as did finer antique shows selling only the very best pieces.

So where are we doing our shopping? Everywhere, in the following outlets.

Antiques Malls

Today one of the most popular places to find your treasure is the *antiques mall,* where as many as several hundred dealers sell their wares under the same roof. Convenience has become a big factor in antiques and collectibles shopping, and the antiques malls have certainly catered to convenience. In fact, malls top the list of favorite spots to shop, and once you've experienced one, you'll know why.

Traveling Shows

The traveling shows, consisting of fine antiques shows, flea markets, specialty shows, and antiques flea markets, do not have a permanent base of operation the way shops do. They commonly operate at fairgrounds, convention halls, or any place where other traveling trade shows occur. If you'd like to find one and don't know how, call the fairground or convention hall nearest your home and ask about any antiques and collectibles shows scheduled in the near future. Check the local chamber of commerce and convention bureau, too. And if these sources don't pan out, call an antiques shop or mall and ask if any good antiques or collectibles shows are coming up. Dealers always know when the best shows take place. Don't forget to check out antiques and collectibles trade papers and magazines. These list shows all around the country (see page 205).

It looked like an old 1960s "bong" pipe used for smoking hashish, or at least that's what the dealer said when he sold this 1000-year-old Turkish water vessel for $10. Handmade and decorated in fine detail, this copper pot may well have been used for carrying and pouring wines and other liquids, too.

A Few Additional Spots

Another place that hunters frequent is the second-hand shop, which offers goods that have been previously used but are not advertised as antiques or collectibles. Garage, rummage, yard, and basement sales are popular, too. And while it is generally assumed that the best of these are found only in rural areas, because people there naturally have houses full of antiques, this simply isn't the case. City sales are just as good, so don't overlook them. Organized sales such as community or town yard sales are also good places to shop; many times, dealers actually rent yards and set up booths.

Accessible Shopping

Most antiques and collectibles venues try to make themselves accessible to people with disabilities because many dealers themselves have mobility difficulties or are disabled. People with physical problems find that being a dealer allows them to set their own hours as well as to sell merchandise indirectly, as in a mall. Accessibility is a more and more important consideration in most places where antiques are sold.

Virtually any traveling show will be accessible, as are most malls and privately owned shops, but there are exceptions — the shops and malls operating in old buildings. If you're traveling to a shop whose accessibility is unknown to you, it's best to call and check instead of arriving only to find that there are too many stairs to climb or that there's no ramp to accommodate your wheelchair. The Americans with Disabilities Act does not require that all buildings be accessible, and one huge exemption is historic buildings. Take heart, though: If you can't get into one shop, there are dozens more with great accessibility just waiting for your visit. And many supersized antiques malls even have wheelchairs available for your use if you don't bring one yourself.

WHY ARE WE SHOPPING?

We shop because we love it. The thrill of the hunt, the excitement of discovery — can it get any better?

But there's more. These days, the reasons people are shopping so avidly for antiques and collectibles are as varied as the shoppers themselves. Consider some of the reasons why hunters spend so much time on the hunt.

- **It's a trendy leisure-time activity.** Everybody's doing it, and with all the new and different places in which old goods can be found, there's something affordable and exciting for almost everyone with an interest or need.

- **It's like a treasure hunt.** You never know exactly what you'll find, or if that thing you desperately need is even out there to be found. When the elements of suspense kick in, looking for antiques and collectibles can become a real adventure, depending on where you're hunting.

- **It's addictive.** Once you've found an $1,800 platinum and diamond Edwardian brooch for $2, you'll keep trying to repeat the amazing feat.

- **It's environmentally correct.** Most people don't consider antiques and collectibles to be recycled goods, but they are. They just happen to have a higher value attached to them than those plastic bottles and aluminum cans you save, separate, and drag to your local recycling center.

- **It's an investment.** Though many antiques and collectibles are good investments, some are not, and it takes an expert to know the difference. That said, good investment-quality antiques can see

A little homework and a quick look in a popular pricing guide, and the dealer wouldn't have stuck this c.1900 brooch valued at $1,800 in a $2 junk box.

tremendous appreciation if the market for them remains constant. But any dealer who guarantees that his merchandise will appreciate is not being honest, and that goes for antiques as well as anything brand new being marketed as collectible. No one knows for sure what will be a hot seller in the future or what will be cold and unsalable tomorrow.

- ◆ **It's a way to buy quality merchandise.** The quality difference between old and new is obvious even to the most inexperienced hunter. Years ago wood veneer was mounted over solid wood instead of being glued to particleboard as it is today. Old kitchen spoons were meant to stir thick, gooey concoctions like homemade chocolate fudge or sugar cookie dough without bending. Vintage fabric was fabric, not a synthetic blend of petroleum products and who knows what else. Go take a look at an old 1930s brass desk lamp, then compare it to a new brass-plated one. Pay close attention to the craftsmanship and detail. Note the price. Compare the weight. See for yourself that old really can be better. Quality is quality no matter what the age, and products created in bygone years are typically higher in quality than much of what's on the market today.

- ◆ **It's a link to your past.** Your childhood toys are there — the ones your mom threw away that are now worth hundreds of dollars. Your grandfather's favorite book is there, along with your grandmother's well-used sewing basket. No, these are not the exact items that were once intertwined in your life, but they are similar and they do evoke good memories. Do you remember sitting next to your

The light from this desk lamp shines as brightly today as it did seventy years ago when it sat atop its first desk. Its brass is solid and heavy, its patina experienced, but if you take one like it home, err on the side of caution and attach a brand new cord.

grandfather while he read to you from that book? Did your grandmother mend your torn shirt, finding the right needle and thread in her sewing basket? It's almost a certainty you will never wander up and down the aisles of any antiques mall without hearing others commenting over and over, "I used to have one of those when I was a kid," or "My mother had one of those, and I haven't even thought about it for years," or "I wonder what ever happened to the one Grandpa had?"

Pause for a moment. Shut your eyes and think about a few of those cherished childhood things: The teddy bear and the fire truck? A china tea service and a Lone Ranger mask? Wouldn't it be nice to find them again?

Nostalgia, according to Webster, is "a longing to go back to one's home, home town, or homeland; a longing for something far away or long ago." Nostalgia exists wherever antiques and collectibles are found.

chapter 2

The Most Popular Spots to Shop

a s you know, antiques and collectibles can be found just about anywhere — behind the haystack in an old barn or sitting right out on a front porch. Great-Aunt Tillie's attic is always a good place to look, too. But most of us don't have access to an old barn, and knocking on a stranger's door asking to look at the wicker chair on the front porch is a little daunting. And about Great-Aunt Tillie's attic . . . it might have been a treasure trove at one time, before your cousins raided it and took everything but the dust bunnies.

Still, Great-Aunt Tillie's attic and a stranger's front porch aside, you're left with many options for your hunt. And with such an interesting and varied array of possibilities, all that's left to do before you rush out the door is to understand a little bit about what they are and how they operate. Knowing how to make a deal in each place you shop is probably something you'll be interested in learning, too.

After all, the time and money you will spend belong to you. Becoming an educated consumer will help you make the most of these precious commodities.

ANTIQUES MALLS

The hottest shopping spot for antiques and collectibles today is the antiques mall, but don't let the name *antiques* mislead you. It's almost a misnomer. These multidealer shops sell everything from antique jewelry and furniture to Beanie Babies to baseball cards, and the variety of what they offer is almost limitless.

On the scene for a couple of decades now, antiques malls were developed as a way for several dealers to share the expense and workload of a single shop. Most people think antiques and collectibles businesses are money-makers, but the opposite is usually the case. Dealers are doing well if they break even, and many are more accustomed to taking a loss than making a profit. Good, salable merchandise is costly; overhead is costly, too. Perhaps the saddest truth for dealers is that many customers are merely browsers who purchase nothing at all or spend only a few dollars for a trinket. Another fact of the business is that because it's rarely lucrative, it's often a part-time endeavor for its dealers. All things considered, the emergence of antiques malls made sense for those trying to make a living selling antiques and collectibles. It was a way to reduce almost every cost except that of acquiring merchandise to sell, and it provided the dealer with a way to have merchandise for sale all the time, even when she wasn't available to sell it herself.

How Does It Work?

The concept of the antiques mall is simple. Several dealers set up their private displays under one roof. Those displays are either open booths in which you are free to walk around and handle the merchandise, or locked glass cases where more expensive or smaller items are shown. The actual owner of the mall charges a monthly rental fee for each space, plus a small commission. He is also responsible for staffing the mall. In some cases, the dealers who rent the space take turns working in the mall to offset rental costs.

Mall Advantages

As the popularity of antiques malls started to grow, so did the size of the stores themselves. The first were small, usually with just a few dealers. Today, however, it's not uncommon to find one with displays from a hundred or more dealers. Some of the largest in the country boast more than four hundred dealers in one building. That's a lot of looking, and walking, for the treasure hunter! Shoppers and browsers love those huge malls because

Don't Take It Personally

Don't be offended if a sales clerk at an antiques mall opens a glass case for you, then stays and watches as you inspect what's inside. Many clerks will even refuse to allow you to remove an item from the case yourself. Instead they'll remove it, then hand it to you. Also, when they see you carrying an item you've decided to buy, they may be quick to take it to the front checkout area for you. Again, don't let that irritate you. It's customary in almost all malls.

The reason for such watchfulness is twofold. First, it's intended to prevent you from dropping and breaking the item. But it also has to do with theft, which is epidemic in all antiques malls, from both customers and other antiques dealers. Small items slip into purses quite easily, and some clever thieves have gotten away with larger things, such as glassware and quilts. Price-tag switching is also a common crime in the malls. So if an employee whisks that item right out of your hands and takes it to the sales area, don't take it personally.

they can idle away a whole day in them without effort; also, if they're on the hunt for a specific item, the chances are much greater of finding it in a mall stocked by two hundred dealers than in one stocked by twenty. Antiques and collectibles hunters are also great bargain seekers, and the large malls give them a chance to do comparison shopping, which is half the fun. Because malls do not set or regulate prices for anything sold, you can find a wide variety of prices for similar or identical pieces. It's conceivable that a Currier and Ives dinner plate selling for $15 in one booth, for instance, is going for $3 in another.

The obvious advantages of shopping a large mall should not discredit the smaller malls. Those attract their patrons, too. In fact, wherever a good mall exists, no matter what its size, there are customers anxious to do some shopping. The key to any mall's success, however, is the quality of merchandise its dealers provide. In other words, the definition of *good* has a huge bearing on whether an individual mall will have staying power or go out of business within a year or two, which many do. *Good*, in terms of an antiques mall, refers to a mall that maintains the quality of merchandise sold. Some malls actually have rules about what can and cannot be displayed in order to keep the mall from looking like a garage sale or general-merchandise flea market. There's nothing more frustrating to a devotee than to drive for an hour to a mall only to find that a better name for the establishment would be *junk store*. The key to an antiques mall's survival and popularity is a good mix of merchandise — many things old, some things relatively new, and all things definitely collectible.

Currier and Ives in any form, whether a framed print or a dinner plate, is a traditional favorite because of its depictions of cozy New England countryside scenes. Currier and Ives dinnerware dating from the 1950s and 1960s is still popular because of its classic look, and it's a great, inexpensive alternative to fine china for almost any dining room table.

Where Is It?

Finding antiques malls is pretty easy, as they are already abundant and their popularity is still growing. Check the yellow pages under the word *antiques* for malls, multidealer shops, and emporiums. When you visit a mall, ask if there is another nearby. Also, check out the information rack located near the entrance to nearly every mall. Antiques malls are friendly with each other and usually have reciprocal deals allowing other shops to leave brochures in the information area in exchange for the same consideration.

Ask other shoppers, too. Normally, if you find a shopper in one mall, you can assume he's been to others. Who better to point you in the direction of another mall than a shopper?

Deal Time

Now, the information you've been waiting for — making a deal. Yes, you can make a deal, even in an antiques mall. The deal probably won't be as good as one you can make face to face with a dealer, but most items in an antiques mall can be discounted a bit. Here is a useful approach to securing a discounted price:

- **Don't ask the sales clerk to offer a discount.** Sales clerks work for the store and do not have the right to discount merchandise belonging to individual dealers. Take note of the booth in which you find an item, however, and ask the clerk if there are any discounts for that booth. You might be directed to a great deal.
- **Pay particular attention to discount signs.** Many booth owners offer sales as a means of getting rid of existing stock to bring in new. Some discounts

may go as high as 50 percent, so look closely, and check for special terms listed on the sign. Red-tagged items may be the only ones for sale right now, or the sale may extend only to items on a certain table or anything made of glass. Whatever the case, sales do go on, so look around. And remember that a sale occurring in one booth or case doesn't mean other booths are offering the sale, too.

- **Be aware that most items over a certain price are eligible for a 10 percent mall discount.** The mall sets the price at which a discount applies, usually on items ranging from $10 to $25 and above, but you have to ask for that discount. It isn't automatic.
- **Don't ask for a discounted price if an item's price tag includes the word "firm."** No discounts whatsoever will apply to that item, so don't bother to ask. The booth owner has given special instructions to the mall owner that the selling price will not be changed from what's marked on the price tag.
- **Seek a deeper discount.** It is possible to seek a discount deeper than the customary 10 percent on pricey items found in antiques malls. The only real disadvantage of shopping a mall is probably the fact that you won't have the opportunity to negotiate with the booth owner face to face. Many malls, however, will act as intermediaries between you and the booth owner, which means that if you really want that $500 kitchen cabinet but can't afford it even with the 10 percent discount, you can make an offer and ask the mall to convey it to the booth owner. If that cabinet has been collecting dust for a year or two, an anxious owner may be willing to accept a reasonable offer, which on the average means about a 20 to 25 percent discount.

◆ **Ask for the rock-bottom price.** Sometimes, though, the dealer simply has too much money tied up in an item to discount it so deeply, so your offer will be rejected. Instead of making a firm offer, however, you can just ask the dealer for her bottom line — "What's the lowest price you will accept for that kitchen cabinet?" You could end up getting it for much less than you would have offered. A collector of pottery vases watched one sit in a mall's glass case for well over two years with a price tag of $175. She loved the vase but wouldn't pay the price, so after drooling over it for so long, she finally asked the mall operator to contact the dealer and find out the bottom line. It turned out to be $89 — just what the dealer had paid for it herself.

Rules That Don't Bend

There are some things you should know when you find the perfect eight-foot-tall armoire for your bedroom:

◆ **You'll have to lug it home yourself.** Antiques malls do not provide delivery service.
◆ **You can't take it back.** All purchases are final; antiques malls don't accept returned merchandise. Thus, it's up to you to thoroughly inspect the piece to make sure it's in acceptable condition and of an acceptable size before you plunk down your money. Otherwise, when you get it home and find it won't fit into your house upright because your ceilings are only seven feet high, you'll have to learn to appreciate the beautiful armoire that sits on its side or lies flat on its back in the middle of the room.

Leave the Plastic at Home

When you make a purchase in an antiques mall, cash and checks are best. Many malls pass along to their customers the 5 percent fee that credit card companies charge the businesses using their services.

Buying "As Is"

Many dealers know their merchandise is damaged but assume a "buyer beware" attitude by not pointing the damage out to the customer. When you're lucky enough to find the words *as is* marked on a tag, take a closer look at what you're buying. *As is* means the dealer is aware of a problem with the piece, and he's letting you know. It's chipped, cracked, or incomplete or has some other flaw. There's nothing wrong with buying a damaged piece, but it should be *your* choice to do so and not something that happens because a dealer is not forthcoming with information, especially when the piece is not returnable.

Do You Love a Good Adventure?

One last item of interest about antiques malls: Be prepared for an adventure when you go shopping. You will find malls operating in barns, brand-new buildings, Victorian houses, old warehouses, abandoned grocery stores, and every other building you can imagine — and probably a few you can't. You may have the experience of riding up and down on an old-time freight elevator, and it may well be electrified. Don't be surprised, however, to step onto it only to find that it was built well before the years of electricity and hasn't been converted. Those old pulley elevators still exist, though you won't have to do the pulling yourself; malls have employees for that. Get used to damp and musty, too. And dusty. You may find yourself plowing through a dark, dank basement or stuffy attic.

If you're lucky, your favorite mall will have a rough room, where many of the discards and collectibles that aren't presentable enough to be allowed into main room displays are stacked in an attic or basement and offered for sale at reduced prices. Rough rooms can be an adventure in themselves, especially if you like rehabilitation projects, because many of the items in these rooms are a do-it-yourselfer's dream come true.

Of course, your favorite mall might turn out to be a brand-new building with the best in old collectibles and antiques. However you find your mall, though, and no matter what type of building it's in, don't miss the adventure. Be prepared to spend hours, or even a day. Many of the larger malls — the ones that will take most of a day to explore — have small cafés and areas that sell refreshments. Some offer vending machines and sitting areas where you can rest your aching feet. Mall operators know you'll be there a while, and they're prepared for your visit, so don't shortchange yourself. Set aside the time, and think of the trip to a mall as a walk through a museum, because in a sense it is. And admission is free.

ANTIQUES FLEA MARKETS

Spending hours wandering up and down the aisles, rummaging through boxes and piles and looking for that perfect picture frame, isn't popular just among those shopping the general-merchandise flea markets anymore. Antiques flea markets have come onto the scene in a big way, and they are wandered and rummaged every bit as much as any other flea market. In fact, they are a favorite among antiques and collectibles hunters because they *are* flea markets and in many ways are much more accessible for the browser and shopper than other outlets. Items are not usually set out in a display with an anxious dealer looking over you, hoping you don't break the piece of porcelain you're examining. As with any other good flea market, merchandise is stacked, crammed into boxes, stuffed under tables, and spilling out into the aisle. And dealers are friendly. They welcome your perusal, even invite it. For the $2 or $3 admission fee these flea markets often charge, it's hard to find a better deal anywhere.

The antiques flea market concept is the same as any other flea market's. Dealers set up displays of items for sale, but these displays are exclusively antiques and collectibles. They aren't usually the finer antiques you're accustomed to seeing in many shops and shows. Instead, they consist of odds and ends; what's offered for sale is as likely to be a vintage piece or a collectible as an antique. The variety of merchandise you can find at any antiques flea market is amazing, though. So are the numbers of dealers. A large show may boast well over a thousand different booths or dealers, and that's a good day's hunting even for the most diligent of antiques and collectibles enthusiasts.

Neither Rain nor Snow

Antiques flea markets are most often located at fairgrounds. They may be held inside a building or out, or a combination of both. Dealers who operate inside buildings pay more for their space and are assured that in the case of bad weather, they will be able to operate without a problem. Outdoor dealers pay less and take their chances, knowing that a thunderstorm will wipe them out for several hours or a day, though a fine drizzle usually won't dissuade too many of their regular shoppers. When winter sets in, however, all the dealers move inside. The show will go on no matter what the time of year because the shoppers will always come.

The Best Times to Shop

There are no standard hours of operation for antiques flea markets. Many operate from sunup to sundown; others follow the traditional nine-to-five routine. Whenever the doors are opened and the dealers shake the sheets off their tables of merchandise, however, it's best to be at the front of the line if you want a shot at the newest selection of merchandise. One of the harsh realities of being a dealer is that most merchandise does not sell quickly, and much of it never sells at all. Regular shoppers often see the same items for sale in their favorite booths month after month, so when a dealer does come up with a fresh stock of collectibles, her booth will be scrutinized and picked over pretty quickly. In the case of an antiques and collectibles flea market, the early bird does get the best worm.

Another great shopping time is near the close of the flea market on its last day of operation. By that time, dealers are tired, they aren't thrilled about having to box up their stock and lug it back home, and they're much

If You Want It, Buy It

When you find it, if it makes your pulse quicken and the price is right, buy it. Don't think about it or wait to see whether you can find another one at a different booth. Don't hide it under a pile of other things so no one else will discover it, then think that you'll come back later. Chances are that the minute you turn your back, someone who's been watching you will get it. Antiques and collectibles hunters are savvy. They observe what people around them are responding to, and when they see someone get excited, they move closer to see what's causing all the fuss. It's a sure bet that if you express a keen interest in something, then put it down, it won't be there when you come back to buy it. It might not even be there when you turn around ten seconds later.

more likely to be agreeable to a deep discount. Also, if the show hasn't been good to them — if they haven't made much money for their three days of effort — they may make a deal that will benefit you more than it will them, in order to walk away with a little cash in their pockets to cover their expenses. Shopping at the end of the show, however, does come with the risk of missing out on buying the old wooden ironing board you had your eye on all day. Someone else may have had an eye on it, too, and beat you to the deal. When you absolutely can't live without it, don't wait. However, if you *can* go home without it and don't mind the suspense of waiting until the last minute, keep an eye on the dealer and make your approach when you see her beginning to pack up.

Prepare Yourself for the Hunt

There is no set way to shop an antiques flea market. Some people prefer a leisurely stroll, stopping at every booth. Others look for those booths selling only specialized merchandise, such as kitchen collectibles or lighting. One thing is sure, though: You'll encounter crowds doing every kind of shopping, and as the day wears on the crowds will increase. By noon your experience could get hectic, depending on how you prepare yourself for it. Consider the following tips when you decide to make a day of it at the antiques flea market:

- **Wear comfortable shoes.** You'll be on your feet most of the day, and many of these venues are so crowded that there's no good place to sit down to take a break. Also, make sure your shoes are good walkers. You could put in a couple of very slow miles by the time you've seen everything you want to.

- **Dress for the weather,** especially if you'll be outside. Since antiques flea markets love to set up in the open air during the summer months, make sure you pack some sunblock. What you may expect to be only a few-minutes walk in the sun could turn out to last several hours. Prepare also for less-than-perfect conditions inside, because indoor antiques flea markets are notoriously hot in summer and cold in winter.

- **Take along a bottle of water and a snack.** Most antiques flea markets have concession stands, but they also have no restrictions about bringing in your own food or beverages. Of course, practicality is best. A lavish spread of fried chicken and potato salad may taste great, but there won't be a place to eat it. Nibbling food as you stroll is a better choice, but don't take food or drinks into a booth. Nothing makes a dealer more nervous than to see someone examining her 1930s white linens while drinking an orange soda. Of course, being forced to buy a 1930s white linen cloth with the big orange stain you just made isn't exactly what you had planned, either.

- **Carry a few grocery bags and something for packing, such as paper towels.** Dealers do have bags and packing materials — usually a motley assortment of things from their homes — but there's no guarantee that what they use will be in good shape. There's nothing more heartbreaking than seeing the depression glass juicer you bought just an hour ago rip through a tiny hole in your bag and shatter. Bring your own grocery bags, double-check them for tiny holes or rips, and double-bag everything you buy. If it's glass, wrap it in paper towels. You may also want to carry a large canvas bag in which to stash several purchases.

♦ When you take the kids with you on your shopping adventure, remember that they're not going to be as enthusiastic as you. In fact, they'll probably be bored, so prepare for that contingency. Pull them in a wagon if they're small enough, and tuck in a few favorite toys to keep them occupied.

Is It Real?

Knowing whether it's authentic, a reproduction (repro), or an all-out fake is tough for many shoppers, and, believe it or not, even the experts get fooled from time to time. Volumes have been written about spotting repros, and many antiques publications regularly print articles on the latest fakes and repros out there. To understand whether something is real, you first need to know the difference between a fake and a reproduction. A *reproduction* is meant to be only a copy of something else; a *fake* is meant to deceive. Knowing this doesn't make it easier to spot a fake or reproduction, and even knowing that an item may not be authentic or old hasn't prevented many a shopper from purchasing it. For the inexperienced eye, distinguishing one from another is tough, but there are a few rules that apply:

♦ **Look for signs of aging and wear.** Turn it over; look at it from all angles. If you think it looks too good to be what it's supposed to be, go with your instincts.

♦ **Don't necessarily believe the engraved maker's marking or label.** Too many violins bearing the old label STRADIVARIUS and pieces of art glass bearing the mark LOUIS COMFORT TIFFANY have fooled buyers for decades.

Fresh squeezed was the way juice was made fifty years ago, and if you'd like to experience some of that homemade freshness today, juicers such as this are available in collectibles and antiques outlets that sell kitchen wares. Just slice an orange in half and place it over the raised part in the middle, then push it down and twist. It's simple, effective, and doesn't require electricity. What will they think of next?

In the early years, we were so busy setting up the United States that we didn't have time to distill fine spirits, so even though we were trying to liberate ourselves from European customs, we still bought their booze. This bottle was full of gin in the late eighteenth century. It was square for easy packing into a wooden case and shipping, hence the name Case Gin.

♦ **Don't always buy into a dealer's story about the object unless she has proof.** Provenance can greatly escalate the value of an item, and unfortunately many dealers invent provenance. A noted antiques bottle expert was shopping a fine antiques show and spotted a bottle that interested him. He knew about the bottle — it was made in the mid-1700s in Europe — but it bore the marks of having spent a century or so at the bottom of an ocean. Since this expert collected bottles salvaged from shipwrecks, he inquired of the dealer, only to be told a long story about how the bottle had a presidential lineage and that the contents had been personally bottled by Andrew Jackson. The dealer justified his triple-market-value price tag with this made-up tale. So when you hear a story to go along with the item of your interest, ask for proof.

♦ **If you're paying only a few dollars, don't worry.** All regular shoppers get fooled occasionally, and a few dollars lost in a bad transaction isn't a big deal. If, however, you're investing a small fortune, ask for a written statement to the effect that if you have the item appraised and it turns out to be something other than what the dealer represented it to be, he will refund your purchase price. Make sure you get accurate contact information from the dealer, since those who work the antiques flea markets move around. If the dealer will not honor this request, don't buy the item.

♦ **Examine the item once again before you make the purchase.** Grab a flashlight and look in the nooks and crannies. Feel the glass for cracks and signs of roughness (feeling is often more reliable than looking). Use common sense. If a glass item has been sitting on a shelf for the past hundred years, there should be signs of wear on the bottom. A two-hundred-year-old table shouldn't be held together with new nails. Everything can be faked or reproduced and, unfortunately, most of today's popular antiques and collectibles are. The bottom line in determining whether it's old or only being passed off as old is that you can't always be sure. Still, do a close check. Trust your instincts. Common sense has saved more than one shopper from making a big mistake. Also, the more experience you gain inspecting items of particular interest to you, the easier it will be to recognize something authentic. (See chapter 6 for more about age and normal wear.)

Let's Make That Deal

You've found just what you've been looking for, and you're fairly confident it's authentic. It's in great shape and it will fit perfectly into your kitchen's decor. The dealer has been keeping an eye on you for the past five minutes and she knows you want it, but she's been standing back, allowing your excitement to mount as you turn it over and over and examine every aspect. You're going to buy it. There's no doubt in your mind, or the dealer's. You've wanted an old cast-iron skillet, and this is the right one, so now it's time to start the negotiation. And yes, you should always negotiate the purchase price when you have the chance. All dealers expect this, and many even factor it into their original asking price.

First, ask the dealer for her best price on that cast iron skillet. She's asking $45, and she'll probably reduce the price by about 10 percent to offer it to you for around $40. That's a reasonable offer on her part, but you may be able to do better. So frown a little. Take in a slow, deep

No, it's not fine crystal, just a fake copy called peanut butter glass because peanut butter was sold in it in the 1960s. Just a decade ago no one was interested in peanut butter glass and it sold for 10¢, but recently it's been rediscovered and the price is on the rise. If you want peanut butter glass, act quickly.

breath and make the dealer wait for a minute while you consider her offer. Keep on sending out the visual clues that you are not satisfied with her offer yet.

Next, make a counteroffer of about 20 to 25 percent below the original asking price. "Will you take $30?" That's a pretty hefty discount, and the answer will probably be no, but the dealer is likely to counter with another offer, because she knows you want that skillet and she's been feeling your money in her pocket from the moment you stepped into her booth. She might ask for $37.50. You'll come right back with, "Will you take $35?" Now she's the one with the scowl on her face, and she'll think for a moment before nodding her head yes. When she's reached her bottom line — "That's as low as I can go" — it's time to buy, if you're serious. Keep in mind, however, that all dealers have a point at which they'll walk away from a deal if they intend to make a profit or at least break even.

Making a good deal is one of the fundamental joys of shopping an antiques flea market. There's no better feeling than walking away with that skillet in hand, knowing you bought just what you wanted and were successful in your negotiations. Occasionally, though, you'll have to walk away empty-handed. The dealer won't budge, or her discount simply won't be enough. If you have to walk away without the skillet, walk. That skillet, or one like it, will probably turn up someplace else.

Even after you've scored a few major discounting successes, don't expect great discounts all the time. Generally, items priced under $10 or $15 don't have much of a profit margin, and you won't see a lot of negotiating on anything so inexpensive. Ask anyway, though. "Can you help me out with the price?" Chances are, you'll get a dollar or two knocked off.

Take a $6 page from an early twentieth-century magazine and a $10 frame from the 1930s, and you have a striking decorative piece for any wall of your home. This 1918 Jell-O advertisement hangs in my kitchen.

What about Untagged Merchandise?

The biggest sticker shock can come on an item that has no sticker. Most dealers are diligent about pricing their items and applying the appropriate labels. If you're perusing a booth and see that everything has a price ticket but the 1933 *Etude* magazine you want to purchase, chances are the ticket came off. This isn't a big deal. Just ask the dealer for the price, then begin your bargaining process. Some dealers never bother putting price labels on their goods, however, and these are the dealers likely to make arbitrary decisions. They'll name a price according to what they think you'll pay. When you've shown a definite interest in the piece, the price you're quoted may be higher than that given to a shopper who shows only a passing interest. If, in the dealer's perception, you appear more affluent than other shoppers, your price may be higher, too. There really is neither rhyme nor reason for some of the deals offered in booths where merchandise is largely unpriced. It's not unusual to ask about a price, then come back hours later to find a different price being offered. Many experienced shoppers never patronize booths with unpriced merchandise.

Some of the best artwork of the early twentieth century is found on old covers of a magazine called The Etude, *meaning "the study." Every cover depicted a musical setting in some form, and piano music in its entirety was found between the covers. From 1900 to about 1940, most serious piano and music students subscribed to* The Etude. *These and other magazine covers make beautiful framed wall hangings. When you find old magazine covers you'd like to display, be sure to put them under glass and keep them away from direct sunlight to prevent damage and fading.*

ANTIQUES SHOWS

Despite the name, an antiques show is just a sale. Sure, there will be antiques for display purposes only, and some of the finer shows even commission the best antiques galleries and decorators to set up entire rooms of antiques just for viewing. But generally, when you see the word *show* attached to antiques and collectibles, you can bet that everything there for show purposes will also be for sale. So don't let the name mislead you, and don't be surprised to find that after you pay your admission, you walk through the doors of an antiques sale. Except at museums and historic points of interest, antiques are rarely just for show.

Antiques shows operate on the same principles as antiques and collectibles flea markets do, except that the price of admission is usually higher than the $2 or $3 you plunked down to get into the flea market. The quality of merchandise is considered better, too. Booths are set up elegantly, instead of in the cluttered flea market fashion, and each booth you enter gives you the feeling of walking into an exclusive antiques store. Special lighting is used to highlight the best objects. Dealers will be more aloof than those you encounter at a flea market. Yes, you will find prices for almost every object displayed, and those prices will generally be much higher than anything you see at the antiques flea markets. But then the goal of the finer antiques shows is to offer you something you'll rarely find in other venues.

A huge "buyer beware" comes with the finer antiques show, as it does with every other antiques and collectibles outlet. Dealers are dealers. Unless they're experts selling an item in their line of expertise, they have limited knowledge — even if the whole package they are presenting looks better than anything you can find elsewhere.

Shows Beget Shows

One of the interesting phenomena associated with antiques and collectibles shows is that shows beget shows. When your fairground is hosting a fine antiques show, chances are you'll also find an antiques flea market in a nearby building, as well as one or two associated specialty shows.

Shows that operate near other shows expect to draw shoppers from the other shows. They also attract dealers who have better-quality merchandise to sell but don't wish to pay the high setup cost of the finer show. Instead, these dealers will pay a lower fee to set up in a nearby antiques flea market or specialty show and count on crowds from the finer shows wandering in. Often they even forgo the expense of advertising because they know the finer shows put on huge advertising campaigns; once shoppers arrive, they'll automatically expect other antiques and collectibles opportunities to exist in the proximity.

Since antiques dealers often price their goods according to the quality of the show in which they're operating, it pays to shop all the shows going on in one area. One prestigious Midwest antique show, put on for the benefit of charity, attracts dealers from throughout the country. The patrons of this particular show are wealthy, and the prices of the merchandise reflect that. Normally, another fine antiques show will follow the charity event to town within a few weeks, bringing back many of the same dealers. Their merchandise, for the most part, is the same as what was offered at the charity affair, but the price tags will have been changed to reflect a different clientele.

Their bottom line is to make a profit. Keep that in mind as you are browsing.

Now that you know the nature of a finer antiques show, do go, if not for the buying experience then at least for the pure pleasure of observing and learning. These are the shows where you will find objects with true provenance on display, and where items are likely to be identified and dated accurately. Many such shows even offer independent appraisal services right on the premises, just in case you have any doubts.

As you shop a finer show, don't forget all the rules you've learned so far:

- **Inspect the merchandise carefully.**
- **Ask if it's authentic and secure a written agreement.** Always request a written agreement stating that your money will be refunded if the item is proven to be something other than what it's represented to be.
- **Ask for a discount.** Many people hesitate to do so at the finer shows because the atmosphere is so different from that in other antiques outlets. You'll walk on carpet instead of cement, listen to the strains of classical music over the public address system, and patronize well-dressed dealers. And yes, for the most part you'll be looking at a different class of goods than you'll find in most other antiques and collectibles venues. Still, the purpose of the finer shows is the same: Dealers come to sell, shoppers come to shop, and browsers come to browse. Same game, different wrapping. That's all.

ANTIQUES AND COLLECTIBLES ON-LINE

On-line outlets are definitely the new kid on the block, and shoppers are flocking to them as an easy way to find just what they want without leaving home. The concept is simple: Dealers list antiques and collectibles for sale on various Internet sites, and shoppers buy them. The most popular type of site is the auction, where you take a look at the picture of something in which you're interested, read the description, then place a bid. Other sites merely display a picture of the object, post a description and price, and wait for someone to purchase it. (See page 205 for a list of popular antiques and collectibles Web sites.)

On-line shopping is convenient if you like the idea of flopping down into your recliner, putting your feet up, and turning on an at-your-fingertips shopping mart. And admittedly, it's an appealing idea. Still, there's a whole string of things you should know before you begin your at-home shopping escapade:

- **Most sales are final.** If you don't like it after the mail carrier drops it on your doorstep, you may well be stuck with it.
- **You won't have the opportunity to inspect an item before you make a bid or purchase.** What you see in the on-line picture is all you'll get. However, in most cases you'll have an opportunity to e-mail the seller to ask specific questions.
- **You may or may not be getting the best price.** This is especially true in an auction, where others are bidding against you. Auction fever can strike, even on-line, and prices can soar out of sight with the push of a computer key or two.
- **You'll be asked to pay by check, money order, or credit card, and your item won't be shipped until payment is received and has cleared the bank.** Most on-line sellers are reputable, but there is nothing to regulate them, so you do run the risk of paying for something you might not receive.
- **It's easy to overextend your stash of money.** Because on-line shopping is simple — and as addictive as home shopping on television to some — it's easy to spend too much, especially when you don't have to dig the cash out of your pocket and hand it over to a dealer as you make the purchase. A few bids here and a purchase or two there add up.

- **Most on-line auctions will hold you to your bid.** Once it's made, it's binding, and you can't back out. There are ways not to buy an item for which you are the high bidder, such as not sending the money to the seller, but many auctions operate on a feedback system: Any negative feedback about you posted by a seller can mean you won't have an opportunity to participate in an auction again. Some on-line dealers even refuse bids from those who have negative feedback posted.

On-Line Warning! Warning! Warning!

The most common complaint heard from regular on-line antiques and collectibles buyers is that the picture of the item was not a good representation. Images can be distorted if a seller doesn't know how to take a good picture and scan it into the computer; colors are often more inaccurate than true for the same reason. The next biggest complaint is that the description was not accurate and the condition of the item — "mint," "near mint," and the like — is misrepresented. Such misrepresentation is called "puffing the wares," and it's an attempt to sell something that can't be inspected in the hope that the buyer isn't savvy enough to know he's been lied to, or to ask for a refund. It's estimated that one-fourth of all on-line purchases fail to live up to their descriptions or pictures. That's a huge figure when you consider that no reputable dealer could afford to have a fourth of her merchandise misrepresented to the public — as soon as knowledge of this spread, she'd be out of business. But it's happening on-line more than it

E-Buyer Beware

Never make an offer or bid on any on-line antique or collectible without first seeing a picture. Most on-line dealers do post photos, and what you see is what you'll get. Others, however, don't make the effort, and what they're offering might be miles away from what you're expecting. E-mail for a picture or ask for it to be sent via snail mail, and if the dealer won't provide one, forget the deal.

should because unscrupulous sellers know buyers are at a clear disadvantage.

On-line auctions and shopping are both experiencing growing pains. Still, there are a few ways to get beyond the obvious problems:

- **Check the seller's feedback from other buyers, if available.** If this feedback is sprinkled liberally with problems and negative comments, don't buy from that seller.
- **Check the seller's return policy.** Demand the statement, "Unconditional satisfaction guaranteed or refund will be issued"; if the seller won't comply, don't buy. Be aware that when you return an item, you will lose the shipping costs you paid and will also be required to pay the cost of returning the merchandise.
- **If you don't receive your money back, contact the on-line company hosting the sale or auction.** Also contact your local postmaster, if you are using the U.S. Postal Service, since deception by mail constitutes a federal crime. And if you have paid by credit card, contact that company and request that they either retrieve the payment or stop it.
- **Make use of escrow accounts, when available.** When you're paying a lot for something, check to see whether the on-line company hosting the sale or auction offers an escrow account, which allows you to send your money to an independent account holder. When you receive the merchandise and are happy with it, the account holder will release payment to the seller. If you aren't happy, you return the merchandise; once it's received, the account holder will release your payment back to you.

- **Leave feedback.** If the on-line antiques and collectibles service offers a means by which you can leave feedback for either the merchandise you received or the overall business transaction, by all means use it. Your negative feedback could save someone else from making a huge mistake, just as someone else's feedback might save you from the same.

Despite its risks, on-line shopping is growing in popularity. Dealers are finding it a relatively inexpensive way to unload merchandise, and for the knowledgeable shopper, there are indeed some deals to be had. But as you wander into the world of cyberspace antiques and collectibles, remember:

- **Set a price limit and do not exceed it.**
- **Know what you're about to make an offer on.** There are many good price and identification guides on the market (see the list on page 205). These can be helpful when you shop any antiques and collectibles venue and aren't sure what it is you're about to buy or what it should cost. Always take a guide with you, but keep it out of sight because it can alert the dealer to a novice circling in for a buy. Dealers love inexperienced buyers. At home, however, you can take the time to check out any item of interest; that dealer out there in cyberspace won't know the difference. So buy a price guide or two and do your homework.
- **In an auction, you won't receive a discount.** If you're doing business with a private dealer who sells on-line, however, you may; so ask.

Buying antiques and collectibles from any of the venues mentioned in this chapter always involves an element of risk, but for some intrepid treasure hunters this risk is part of the thrill of discovery. And it *is* a thrill to find, at the antiques flea market, the perfect little stool to set next to the washer in your laundry room, or some old railroad lanterns to hang above your family room fireplace. If you haven't gone out to have a look at what's for sale, do it. You don't have to buy a thing. Spend some time. Browse. Compare. Get a hands-on feel for what you might want. And if you choose on-line shopping, spend some browsing time there, too. Compare. Ask sellers for more detail. Those who do their browsing, study, ask questions, read the guides, and learn are the ones who find the best deals. Most libraries have dozens of volumes on antiques and collectibles, so start your adventure there.

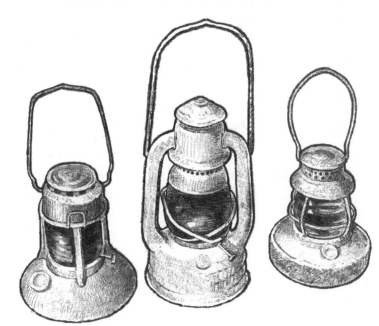

Whether you're a railroad enthusiast or someone looking for an additional light source to hang in the family room next to the fireplace, an old railroad lantern might be just what you need. They look great, particularly in a rustic setting, and their light shines so brightly that they could still usher a train into the station, which is how they were originally used.

chapter 3

More Great Shopping Opportunities

h unting for your treasure is fun, and you don't have to stick to the most popular places to find that old hutch that's been the object of your search for the past year and a half. It may well be lurking in the corner of a garage with a FOR SALE sign hanging on it, or it could be stuffed behind three rows of furniture waiting to be auctioned. Look out on a neighbor's curb on heavy trash pickup day. You might even find it there.

Because of the popularity of the antiques and collectibles venues listed in chapter 2, many people don't consider shopping the tried-and-true outlets that were once just as popular — and often the only places to look. So how long has it been since you've meandered through a secondhand store? When was the last time you spent a Friday or Saturday afternoon going from yard sale to yard sale? Years ago, these were great places to find that treasure, because most of the merchandise coming into the hands of the shop operators was set out for sale without much scrutiny. Then, an original Picasso was discovered at a garage sale, and Christopher Columbus's map, with his and Queen Isabella's signatures, turned up in a stack of old newspapers at a Salvation Army store. These days, secondhand junk is looked at pretty closely before it goes up for sale. This doesn't mean you won't find great antiques and collectibles at these places, nor does it mean you won't be the one to buy a $40 million Picasso for a couple of bucks. What it does mean is that the likelihood of finding high-quality collectibles in a traditional secondhand store isn't as great as it was several years ago. Don't forgo the pleasure of some of the less popular or offbeat opportunities, though. If you're in the market for a 1940s chrome toaster rather than an 1840s European oil lamp, you may just have some great luck.

INDEPENDENT SHOPS

There's something quaint about a dark, dusty shop owned by an eccentric little old man. The shelves are stacked high with everything from fishing tackle to century-old photos to salt and pepper shakers, and what looks like clutter to you is really quite organized to the owner.

Such places still exist, but their owners are finding the burden of operating a small independent shop more difficult as each year passes. Small shop owners have to pay their overhead costs single-handedly; also, the expense of finding and buying antiques and collectibles to resell is escalating, and profit margins are decreasing. Another thing that's really hurting small dealers today is that shoppers visit their establishments only as a second thought, and only if the shops are located in a cluster of other stores or near an antiques mall. A shop that's miles off the beaten path stands little chance of huge success these days because serious shoppers have become convenience shoppers, and there's nothing convenient about

These oil lamps, c. 1840, are still as functional and as easy to use today as they were when they were created. Blown by a little old glass maker in Russia, they sat on a family mantel and were used on a daily basis for 150 years. Today they are retired from day-to-day duty, but they do light up beautifully for old-times' sake and on special occasions and Russian holidays.

driving fifty miles just for the experience of browsing that tiny curio shop.

One independent shop owner of twenty-five years finally closed his doors. He was the only antiques and collectibles dealer in his tiny town, and while his storefront was prominent on the town square, days would go by when he wouldn't see a customer walk through his door. Also, because his shop was twenty miles from the nearest mall, shoppers rarely bothered to make the trip. His chief complaint, however, was not his lack of business but the difficulty of purchasing different items for resale. Such buying required trips that took him out of town for days at a time, forcing him to close up his own shop; the cost of his trips nearly ate up his profits. Finally the dealer tacked an OUT OF BUSINESS sign in his window, boxed up his merchandise and carted it over to the mall, and did what many other dealers are doing these days: He became a mall booth owner at a fraction of the cost and physical effort it took to run his own shop. His greatest benefit was reduced business overhead, which enabled him to mark down his prices. This, in turn, was responsible for creating more yearly profit from his mall venture than he'd seen from his own shop in several years.

Hardships aside, the small shops do go on. They operate in every manner of building, and often you'll find an old sign tacked to a fence post indicating antiques for sale in a private residence, barn, or shed. Stop and look when you see such an advertisement, but be prepared for the higher prices you'll probably find. Small, independent shop owners are solely responsible for all the costs of running their business, and this is reflected in the prices they ask for their merchandise. It has to be, if they want to cover their expenses and still make a small profit.

Shopping

There is no difference between the way you go about shopping in a small store and the way you browse any other venue where antiques and collectibles are for sale. You do have the advantage of dealing with the owner directly, and this helps when it comes time to make a deal. Other than that, all the usual shopping rules apply:

- **Take your time and browse.**
- **Inspect the merchandise carefully.** Don't be afraid to let the dealer know that an item is chipped or otherwise broken, if you discover it to be. Many things get handled and damaged by customers, and shop owners are not always aware of this.
- **Ask questions.** Don't be embarrassed if what you're asking seems silly.
- **Ask for a discount.**
- **Ask if there's similar merchandise.** If the water pitcher you've found is close to what you want but not quite perfect, ask the dealer if he has any similar pitchers. Your treasure could be in another aisle or stored in the basement. Dealers are notorious pack rats who often have boxes and boxes of merchandise stacked out of the way, unopened.
- **Make a special request.** If you really want something the dealer doesn't have, ask her if she can get it. You'd be surprised what a dealer can lay her hands on when she knows she has a buyer.

Antiques are sold everywhere you go, and when you're lucky enough to find an out-of-the-way sign leading you down the road less traveled, invest a few minutes to drive those miles and you may just find that proverbial pot of gold at the end of your journey.

Selling Your Treasures

Small-shop operators not only sell antiques and collectibles but buy them, too, and they love it when people approach them with good, resalable merchandise. There are several things you should know before you decide to sell Grandpa's collection of old wooden planes, however.

- **Always offer goods to a dealer who sells similar merchandise.** One who specializes in jewelry is unlikely to buy a collection of old tools.
- **Don't expect to receive book value.** Price guides will help you determine value, but a dealer will rarely purchase anything for market value; there would be no room for his own profit. If the plane's book value is $100, for example, don't expect to receive that much for it.
- **Don't accept the first price offered by the dealer.** This price is usually much less than half the book price. If the dealer offers you $25 for the plane, counter the offer with $75, then try to work yourself into a compromise somewhere in the middle. Half the book value is probably what you can expect to receive for the plane after the dealing is done, but if you want to avoid the offer–counteroffer exchange altogether, just set a price and ask for it. Be prepared for the dealer to try for a better price, anyway.
- **Don't feel obligated to sell an item to a dealer if you don't like the offer he's making.** Take it somewhere else. Every antiques dealer is on the lookout for great things to sell.

Grandpa White's planes were simple, but they smoothed out the surfaces of some beautiful handmade walnut furniture. Today, old planes like these are popular collectibles, especially for newer-generation carpenters, and while they look wonderful on display, they can still perform their original function.

Repeat Customers

There are advantages to being a customer with whom the dealer has become acquainted. You'll often get much better discounts, and sometimes you'll be granted access to the newest merchandise before it goes on sale to the general public. You can also leave your wish list. A dealer who knows you'll come back and buy from her over and over is more likely to hunt for the items on the list than one who doesn't know you.

One avid jewelry collector found a tiny shop selling lovely Victorian pieces. Much of the jewelry bore high prices, but the collector splurged about once every two months and bought something. After several purchases, the discounts she received started to increase, until she was finally being offered almost 30 percent off. The collector kept her eye on a particularly expensive brooch for quite a while, but even with a deep discount it was well out of her price range. After almost a year of wistful sighs every time she looked at the piece, though, she finally had the opportunity to purchase it: The dealer dropped to his lowest possible offer and even agreed to let her make monthly payments. All this happened only because she was one of his regular customers. In the end, the dealer didn't make a penny's profit on that transaction, but he did cement a relationship that will guarantee him frequent sales for as long as he keeps his doors open.

GENERAL FLEA MARKETS

Yes, you can find the goods at flea markets not specifically selling antiques and collectibles. You'll have to be a little more discerning, however, because general flea market dealers probably won't be able to tell you much more than "it's old." In other words, it's up to you to know what you're buying. Of course, if you like it, if it has a place in your home, and if the price is right, what the dealer knows or doesn't know won't matter.

Shopping

Shopping a general flea market — where you'll find everything from brand-new sweatshirts and incense burners to vintage furniture, secondhand VCR tapes, and outdated food products — is much like shopping an antiques flea market. The same strategies apply:

- You *can* receive a discount.
- The best time to arrive is at the start of the sale.
- Larger discounts are often available as the show is beginning to close.
- Dealers don't necessarily know everything, or even anything, about the merchandise they are selling.

Even so, general flea markets can be great places to do your hunting, because many of their dealers do sell a little bit of everything. Granted, the hunt may take longer since you are plowing through mounds of items that don't even come close to qualifying as collectibles.

One huge advantage, though, is that because the dealer sells in high volume and variety, he may be sitting on several sleepers without knowing it. That $1,800 platinum and diamond brooch a collector found for $2 (see chapter 1) came from a general flea market, where a dealer had set out a box of junk jewelry with the sign EVERYTHING IN THE BOX $2 EACH.

Everything
in the box
$2 EACH

Making the Deal

Deals can be made a little differently at a general flea market, because often a dealer operates only in terms of making a profit based on what she paid for the item. Antiques and collectibles dealers are notorious for wanting full market value on most pieces they sell, even if they paid only $5 for an item valued at $100. General flea market dealers, however, are more often satisfied with a reasonable profit margin and are willing to sell a piece for a smaller price that reflects what they actually paid for it. This is good for you, especially if you have some knowledge about the item you're seeking.

One well-known junk dealer in a midwestern town sets up rows and rows of unpacked boxes and posts the sign: 5 ITEMS FOR $5, THE 6th FREE. FIRM! He buys box lots from auctions, yard sales, estate sales, and anyplace he can get them, including other flea market booths, and he pays just $5 for each box of odds and ends he purchases. He knows that this $5 can turn into about $50 if most of a box's items sell, and he's happy with that profit margin. Because his flea market display consists of several hundred boxes, he doesn't bother to go through everything, and he knows he may well pass up a sleeper from time to time. But when he weighs the time it would take him to sort through his tens of thousands of items for one or two sleepers against the profit he *knows* he'll make, he's content to sit back and let the shoppers have their way with his merchandise. And they do. People line up to take a shot at his box lots, and there's a general frenzy when he announces, "On your mark, get set, go shop!" over his bullhorn at the beginning of his sale. Hardly a shopper walks away empty handed. After all, who can pass up five items for $5, plus a freebie?

Leave No Stone Unturned

Don't overlook any booth at a general flea market — even if it seems to be selling only new goods or goods that don't interest you. Many dealers do have a few old things to sell, maybe from their own garage or their Great-Aunt Tillie's attic. No dealer will pass up the opportunity to sell something if there is profit to be made.

Yard Sales

In the context of this book, the term *yard sale* includes basement sales, garage sales, and anything that comes out of a house to be sold on the premises. Hopeful sellers often tack signs on telephone poles, place ads in local papers, post notices on grocery store bulletin boards, and do just about anything to draw in the crowds that will buy the household items and clothing they no longer want.

There are actually three types of sales that can fall under the general term *yard sale,* and each has unique characteristics.

General Yard Sales

These are the most common, and they usually occur when someone is cleaning out a house trying to get rid of clutter. Typically, the general yard sale season starts in spring and extends into autumn, but summer is a popular time for most sellers because they've completed their spring cleaning and boxed and bagged everything they want to get rid of.

As you learned in chapter 1, yard sales are usually held on weekends, often running on Friday and Saturday or Saturday and Sunday. The more successful ones rarely operate for more than two days, and some even set up for only one; if you see a sale advertised that sounds promising, keep its short duration in mind. And get there early. Yard sales are hugely popular today, because there is so much interest in buying vintage goods, and dealers as well as shoppers are flocking to them. Be aggressive in your shopping, too. Most dealers are, and they're the ones who usually walk away with the best treasures. So grab it and don't let it go if you think you'll buy it. Chances are that if you think it's good enough for you to take home, someone else will want to take it home, too.

Shoppers flock to good yard sales because they believe these are the places where the best deals can be found. Perhaps the old trivet is for sale for a few dollars because the owner doesn't know its true value. Maybe the antique candy dish has an unbelievably low price tag because the owner didn't realize it was an antique. Or the tarnished silver bowl might be sterling, and the owner just didn't recognize its mark. Whatever the case, savvy shoppers and dealers know sleepers can be found in yard sales, and their prices are usually surprisingly low — well below anything you'll find in other antiques and collectibles venues. And yes, you can make a deal. Ask for a discount, by all means.

Standing Yard Sales

Some yard sales seem to be up and running every time you blink your eyes. These are actually secondhand businesses thinly disguised as yard sales. On a regular basis, their operators drag out the tables and set up the displays, and if you look closely, you'll see the same items for sale time after time.

Many states are catching on to these operations and are beginning to regulate them with the laws and taxes applied to regular businesses.

Just a few tips about standing sales:

- Prices are often higher than those found in other yard sales.
- Great deals and discounts are not as common.
- Merchandise may not be from the home, as you would expect, but from other secondhand sources. Inspect it carefully.

One person's yard sale junk can be another's treasure. All of these items found at a yard sale date from the 1930s and are worth about $75 each, but the silver-plated candy dish (left) sold for $10, the trivet (center) cost $12, and the small bowl (right) had a $1 price tag on it. A savvy shopper at this sale could have turned a $23 investment into $225 in less than a minute, and that's the kind of deal about which every serious investor dreams.

Community and Organization Sales

Shopping at a sale organized by several different parties can be almost like shopping at an antiques mall. The variety of merchandise is large, the prices good, and the crowds huge, especially if the sale has been publicized. And most large sales are advertised.

The reason behind the community sale is to appeal to avid shoppers who want the convenience of ten or twenty yard sales in a row, or who prefer to shop a huge sale, such as one held by a church or charitable organization. Some communities go even farther, however, and turn their sales into events. For example, Fairhaven, Ohio, is a tiny town consisting of a dozen or so houses in an out-of-the-way valley. There's really nothing in the town, even though the setting is quaint and the buildings old. But on the first weekend of every June, Fairhaven transforms itself into a whole-town antiques and collectibles yard sale. Dealers troop in from all around the country, renting yards, driveways, weedy lots, and every inch of space available. Tens of thousands of shoppers follow.

Fairhaven is a successful venture because its dealers offer quality merchandise and its shoppers know what to expect. Also, the effort to fill all available space with shopping opportunities is an antiques and collectibles hunter's dream — and it comes true yearly.

For any community or organized sale, arrive early. Inspect everything you intend to buy because you probably won't be allowed to return merchandise. Also, when you shop a sale involving several sellers, discounts can apply if you are dealing with the owner of a particular booth. If, however, you're shopping a rummage sale run by a church or some other organization trying to raise money, discounts are not usually given, since the merchandise comes from the donations of many different people.

Secondhand Stores

Secondhand stores can be anything from shops that sell exclusive vintage bridal gowns for $1,500 to junk stores offering everything you can imagine for $1.50. Typically, when you think *secondhand*, you conjure up the image of thrift stores such as Salvation Army, Goodwill, and AMVETS. Many churches operate thrift stores, too. They collect used merchandise and sell it to fund their organizations, and their mainstays are clothing, furniture, and household items.

There really is no right or wrong way to shop a secondhand outlet. You simply find the item you want to buy, inspect it to make sure it isn't damaged or that it's exactly what you want, and make your payment. Discounts are rarely accepted — except, perhaps, in privately owned stores — and merchandise is not returnable.

When antiques malls and other antiques and collectibles outlets became popular, the popularity of traditional secondhand stores dwindled. Today, however, as vintage clothing is becoming more and more trendy, secondhand stores are becoming the *in* places to shop for those who want to achieve a certain look. And as new generations are finding their look in these stores, they're also finding their toasters, dinner plates, and kitchen chairs. If you haven't taken a look in a good secondhand store lately, maybe it's time to go back and rediscover what so many are discovering for the first time.

Auctions

Auctions are really in a category all by themselves. They're extremely popular with dealers, but less so with individuals looking for good buys at great prices because there are few, if any, deals to be made in most auctions, and discounts are not offered. Prices can go quite high if there is strong interest in a specific piece or if a bidder has a compulsion to win, no matter the cost. Some final selling prices make no sense at all and can only be attributed to bidding run amok. And bidders often do get caught up in the bidding process to the exclusion of common sense. For example, bidding for one set of three old, stained feather pillows in the traditional blue-and-white-striped ticking was started at $1, and you knew these pillows were not particularly desirable because the auctioneer hated to touch them. People bid, however, and in the end the pillows sold for over $50. The lucky winner didn't feel so lucky after she took a closer look at what she bought, and later she admitted that the object was more to win the bid — she hated to lose — than it was to own those nasty old pillows. Incidentally, the whole set went into the trash can sitting under the auction house's EXIT sign.

Even with the peculiarities surrounding auctions, and many of their bidders, they can be great places to find just what you need or want, and there are several way to make your auction adventure successful. The first is to know what type of auction you're attending.

Consignment Auctions

CONSIGNMENT AUCTION
A sale where the sellers pay a commission to have their items sold.

Anyone can leave merchandise to be sold at an auction house; it's called *consignment,* meaning other people do the selling. They'll charge the seller a commission for making the sale, and they'll quite often tack a 10 percent commission onto the buyer's total bill as well. Don't be surprised to see this add on. One reason it happens is that many auction houses actually buy and sell their own merchandise, and while a standard commission from the seller is always built into a sale, when the auction house is selling its own items there is no commission to be had. Hence, that extra amount is passed on to you.

Virtually everything will turn up at consignment auctions. These are always buyer-beware situations, because unless you're attending an exclusive auction that does its own authentication and appraisal, there are no regulations about what will be sold. And auctioneers have discovered that a buying frenzy can be created around almost anything, including a bunch of stained pillows. They're masters at creating that frenzy: They can intimidate, embarrass, and coerce you into bidding and raising your bid. These tactics are not ruthless, just good business, so it's up to you to make sure that your end of the deal ends up well, too.

When you attend a consignment auction, keep these suggestions in mind:

- **Arrive early and inspect the merchandise on which you might bid.** Good auctioneers know about any problems with the piece they're about to auction and will usually point these out, but chips and cracks can be missed. Do the inspection yourself before you consider bidding.
- **Set your bidding limit and don't exceed it, not even by a few dollars.** A few dollars on top of your set price — plus a few more on top of the bid that came after it — add up quickly, so exercise some willpower. Write down what you're willing to spend and keep reminding yourself just where you'll stop when the bidding starts climbing.
- **Many consignments come with a reserve.** This means they won't be sold for anything less than a specified preset dollar amount. For example, a

nineteenth-century washstand may come with a reserve of $350, which means it can't be sold for anything less than that price, even if the highest bid is $340, only $10 under.

- **Don't bid on something you don't want.** If you've purchased one Oriental rug and another comes up, a good auctioneer will come back to you for a bid even if you've shown no interest in the rug on the auction block at the moment. He may stop the auction for a few seconds and coax you to bid, then come back and ask you to raise your bid every time someone else chimes in. Inexperienced auction-goers often succumb to this tactic, but don't let the auctioneer persuade you. Just shake your head no every time he approaches you.

- **Listen carefully.** Auctioneers are notorious for selling several similar or identical items at one time. You may be bidding on the whole box of pots and pans when you think you're bidding on only one. Conversely, you could think you've just won the bid for the whole box when you've only won the bid for one pan. If you're in doubt, don't raise your hand to ask the question, because that could be construed as a bid. Be brave, and just shout it out. Listen carefully to the bid increments, too. Auctioneers are masters at changing them without anyone noticing, but if you have the opportunity, it's perfectly acceptable to shout out your own bid instead of bidding what the auctioneer suggests.

- **Don't believe everything you hear.** Even if the auctioneer says it's a genuine Tiffany, it could be a genuine Tiffany repro. Auction houses advertise their most valuable antiques because such advertising will bring in dozens of experienced dealers who'll pay top dollar. So if you see an authentic Tiffany bring a bid of only $200, remember this: Low bids on seemingly rare or pricey pieces are a big tip-off that the piece probably isn't what it seems.

- **Request that items be moved up.** If you've waited three hours and it looks like that unusual 1950s lamp you want isn't even in line to go on the block yet, ask to have it moved up. All auction houses employ helpers who actually take the bids and move the items into place to be auctioned. Make your request known to one of these helpers.

Auction Warning

When an auction house owns the item up for bid, it will do whatever it takes to keep the bidding high, including creating a phantom to bid against you. If you make a bid and someone ups it — but you're not quick enough to see who — be aware that this is probably the auctioneer's attempt to get more money for the seller, which in this case is the house.

Estate Auctions

An estate auction is handled, in practice, much the way a consignment auction is, but all items come from a single estate, usually that of a person who has died. Estate auctions happen for several reasons:

- The family of the deceased is trying to dispose of the items.
- The will has stipulated an equal split of the estate to family members without specifying who gets what. The only way to settle such a matter is often to sell everything at auction, then divide the money accordingly.
- The deceased died without a will or there are no legal inheritors, and the state, as inheritor, is seeking to turn the estate into cash.
- An entire estate has been left to an organization, such as the Humane Society, and the organization must turn the assets into cash.

In rare cases, estates are auctioned off before the owner has died. One reason for this is to reap the benefits of the money. Another is specific to antiques and collectibles dealers and collectors: They've spent a lifetime gathering treasures and may want to convert their collections into retirement funds. No matter what the reason for the auction, though, anything advertised as *estate* usually draws large crowds. Most people expect estate pieces to be of better quality than the things found at consignment auctions.

Estate auctions are like consignment auctions in most aspects, but they differ in several ways:

- If there's room, the auction may be held on the estate premises. It can be held at the auction house, too, depending on space and parking limitations on site.
- Generally, there are no reserves. Often, in auctions where reserves are allowed, many pieces are not purchased because the reserve price wasn't met. In auctions with no reserves, everything is sold.
- Bidding wars are common if family members want a certain piece that wasn't provided for in the will. Prices can go extremely high when a family heirloom is involved, so exercise caution in your own bidding if you get the feeling you're coming between two brothers who want the same piece. Their intent is to own that precious family heirloom, and often price is not a consideration when it comes to the rights of ownership.
- If it's advertised as an *estate tag sale*, the auctioneer has appraised the items and tagged them with selling prices. The price is what he would expect to receive if he were to auction the items. You can simply pay the tag price if you'd rather avoid the auction ordeal.

RESERVE
The minimum price for which an item can be sold at auction.

Strategies for Any Auction

Some rules apply at both estate and consignment auctions:

- **Bring cash.** Checks may be acceptable, too, but usually you must be preapproved to pay by check.

- **Don't jump at an opening bid.** Auctioneers always start high, hoping an inexperienced buyer will get suckered in, but after the opener is ignored, the next bid will probably drop to a reasonable level. However, some experts advise avoiding the second bid, too, in case it's still elevated a bit.

- **Don't get caught up in body-movement bids** like raising the left eyebrow, puckering your lips, scratching your head. Imagine what will happen if you really do have to scratch your head during the bidding: You may inadvertently bid $10,000 on an old pump organ you don't even know how to play. Instead, use the number card you'll be given when you sign up to bid. Hold it high in the air, wave it if you have to, and make sure one of the auction employees sees it. Call out "over here" if no one does. Your number card is much better than that old wiggle-your-nose maneuver.

- **Pay promptly, and take your purchase with you.** Most auction houses are prepared for the contingency that you've spent much more than you have with you, and they will allow you to return within one or two days to make payment. With few exceptions, though, they will expect you to cart your merchandise off the lot once you own it. Remember this when you're bidding. If you can't get that china closet into your two-door hatchback, you'd better have a backup plan ready.

Curbside Coups

For the really brave of heart, there are treasures to be found sitting on the curbs, waiting to be hauled off by the trash collectors. Dumpsters are another great source, if you don't mind jumping into other people's trash.

It's amazing what people will throw away. Some toss it out to be truly rid of it; others do so because they know there are hunters out there who will find it and take it home. And many of those Dumpster divers and curbside collectors have regular routes that net them amazing things. One Dumpster diver indulges every weekend and as often during the week as he can. He furnished a new house with great collectibles that others have pitched; those items for which he had no use went into storage and materialized at a garage sale that earned him a couple of months' worth of house payments. His cost was a little time, but no money.

Another curbside observer couldn't believe her eyes when a neighbor pitched an old Mission-style oak desk. It dated to the early twentieth century and was worth hundreds of dollars. But it was stacked to be hauled off with the trash. Needless to say, the trash collectors didn't get it.

Raiding a Dumpster or grabbing discards from the trash certainly isn't everyone's idea of antiques and collectibles hunting, but many people do both, including dealers. And there are some great finds to make if you're not too embarrassed to make them.

Curbside Collection Tips

If you think you'd like the thrill of the Dumpster or the excitement of grabbing something from a curb, make sure you know the trash pickup schedule. Much of the best stuff gets set out the night before. Also, raiding the trash is a competitive practice, so don't be surprised to find other marauders out there with you on your midnight hunt. They know when and where to find the good things, too.

Getting a Feel for What You Need

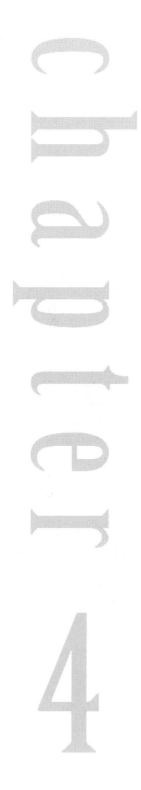

S hopping for the things that appeal to you is one of the best parts of acquiring antiques and collectibles for your home. But what if you're an inexperienced buyer, or you're on a tight budget? How do you know just what you should buy, or even how to get yourself organized enough to take that first step? Often a simple plan is all you need. You don't have to be an expert to know what you like, need, or want, and you certainly don't have to approach your first shopping venture with an armoire full of expertise. What you do need is a feel for what you intend to accomplish, and that's where your own personal plan will come in handy.

START AT THE BEGINNING

No, it's not time to go out and start your shopping yet. There are several steps to consider before you get to that point, but climbing them can be just as much fun as the actual shopping you'll do later on. Each step will prepare you for that moment when the antiques mall doors open and you're the first in line, armed with a wish list in one hand and checkbook in the other. So go grab some paper and a pen, then prepare to start with a little homework.

You Don't Have to Be an Expert, But...

Knowing something about what you'd like to buy is a good way to get started, and there are several ways to accomplish this. First, consider finding a few books at the library or in a bookstore. Books have been written about every category of antiques and collectibles known to humankind — along with a few categories no one knew people were seriously collecting. When you're in the process of setting up your kitchen, for example, try to find and read several of the dozens of books written about kitchen collectibles. The writers are experts and their knowledge will be invaluable to you in your attempt to learn about whatever treasures you're seeking.

Next, go browsing. Leave the checkbook at home, but go ahead and take a few hours to look at everything *kitchen* you can find in several malls, shops, or flea markets. Take notes, including descriptions that are accurate enough to help you find a similar item in one of the books you're reading.

After you've spent the day looking at kitchen utensils, go home and study your books again. See if you can find information on any of the pieces you've seen or included in your notes, then compare what you've recorded with what the experts are telling you. It's almost a sure bet that after you've spent hours looking at old utensils, plus several more reading about them, you'll have a much better feel for what you want when it comes time to do your shopping. Still, the biggest advantage to doing your homework — in other words, looking before you leap into an investment — will be the financial savings that inevitably come with knowledge. You might not think $10 for a circa-1930 stirring spoon

Browsing Tips

Make the most of your browsing. Take notes on an object, so you'll have something to refer to later. Include:

- ◆ Size
- ◆ Color
- ◆ Material from which you think it might be made
- ◆ Identifying marks, such as a maker's name or logo
- ◆ Any dates or initials on the object
- ◆ Asking price
- ◆ Any information or provenance the seller is including with the object

is a tremendously high price to pay the first time you see it. When you've seen identical spoons selling for $5 in several places, however, and you've done enough homework to know they're probably not worth more than that, this little bit of expertise will translate in a few extra dollars in your pocket — dollars you can use to buy an old ice cream scoop, measuring cups, or another stirring spoon.

More Homework

Browsing is a truly fun assignment to tackle, one any antiques and collectibles devotee would love to do anytime, anywhere. But browsing can be taken to another level that's completely outside the shops, shows, and malls where you'll eventually do your buying. Some of the most outstanding testaments to the lifestyle of days gone by can be found in museums or historic homes and buildings. These can be found almost anywhere, but if you don't know of any close to you, call your local historical society. They will be able to put you on a statewide historic trail that could turn out to be as exciting as it is rewarding. And when you find an historic site or museum, the few dollars you'll pay for admission will treat you to an authentic walk through the past. Often, you'll be allowed to snap pictures, but if not, ask for printed materials or a source for a few postcards with pictures of rooms that hold particular interest for you in your quest to set up your own rooms.

One of the great things about touring historic homes is the chance to see an entire room put together in the style of a particular period. You may be able to view a kitchen in context instead of viewing just a few iron utensils like the ones you've seen on display in antiques

You're sure to get $10 worth of stirs out of this 60-year-old spoon, and if you're pressed for time or you're happy with the price, there's no reason not to pay a little more than book value. But with some comparison shopping, you could actually reduce your cost per stir by half, and that's a good value by any homemaking standard.

shows. And if you're lucky enough to be touring a living history museum — an historic site where lifestyle and observances of the day are reenacted — you'll be able to witness just how the forged iron ladle was used, instead of guessing.

Another great reason to visit an historic house or display is that the curator is usually loaded with information specific to the area or period depicted at the site. She knows the way things went together and how and why they were used. If you want to know how the oil lamp was lighted, don't hesitate to ask. You might just receive a personal demonstration.

Museums are another great link to the past. Those with antiques, period furniture, and household items on display would certainly be your best source of ideas about the kind of decorating you'd like to do, but more often than not you'll encounter a museum of art, not of historic objects. And if you're asking yourself what a museum of art can do to help you in your quest to set up a vintage kitchen, the answer is simple. Look at the background in those paintings. Artists painted scenes typical of their day, and those who painted in 1940, or 1840, just might have included some details in their artwork that can make your research easier.

In the same vein, take another trip to your library for some vintage books and magazines — the ones actually produced *in* the period that interests you, not *about* that period. Here are some tips for your library journey:

- If your ideal kitchen is straight from 1940, locate some circa-1940 magazines, either intact or on microfilm, and find pictures that featured kitchens.
- Ask your librarian about noncirculating or archival volumes kept out of the hands of the general public.

- In larger libraries, you'll probably find several circulating books from 1940 that will have helpful pictures. Try cookbooks, for instance, or home decorating references.
- Check out some movies made in that era, then pay close attention to the background detail.
- Don't forget about old catalogs as a source of good information. Copies of early twentieth-century Sears catalogs are still around. Many are even being reproduced.

MAKE A WISH BOOK

Shopping without giving much thought to what you want or need can be quite fun, especially if you have an unlimited budget and unlimited space in which to place your purchases. Planning, however, is the way to go if you feel the constraints of money or space, and one of the best ways to plan what you'd like to buy is to create a wish book. Quite simply, it's a scrapbook of pictures and ideas. You can use clippings from magazines, snapshots, your personal rendition of something you like, or photocopies from antiques books. You can also include notes you write to yourself about the dresser you saw at a flea market that might work in your bedroom, or the tiny chair you'd like to find to fit into a space in your hallway. However you design your wish book, though, there are some simple ways to make it work for you.

The Room-by-Room Wish Book

One of the best ways to approach your wish book is to create a separate section in it for each room you wish

Specialized Libraries

You may be able to find the information and resources you are looking for at a specialized library. Visit a university library. If it's an old university, you might find hundred-year-old volumes right on the shelf. Also, ask the curator of a local history museum or a director of your local historical society if they have a private library you could access; many do. Such libraries often aren't open to the public, but sometimes all it takes is a simple request to be allowed in.

to decorate. Then, as you put together each section, ask yourself the following questions:

Floors
- Are they carpeted?
- Are they hardwood? Does the wood need work?
- Do you need throw rugs or a larger area rug?
- Do you intend to leave the floors as they are?
- What is the total floor space for the room, and how much will be available for collectibles?

Walls
- Are they in good shape?
- Do they need a coat of paint or new wallpaper?
- Are there any blemishes you intend to conceal?
- Will the color scheme change or stay the same?
- Have you considered some of the historical paint colors available today? What about stenciling?
- Will existing wall hangings stay or go?
- How much total wall space is there, and how much of it will be available for vintage wall hangings you intend to purchase?
- How much wall space is occupied by existing furniture, and how much will be available for what you intend to buy?

Ceiling
- What is your ceiling's height?
- What is its texture?
- Is it in good shape?
- Does it need a coat of paint?

Windows
- Is the light direct or indirect? Vintage fabrics and paper collectibles don't fare well in direct sunlight.
- Will your curtains or drapes stay, or do you intend to change them?

Lighting

- Is the lighting adequate or will more be added?
- How much light does this room need?

Upkeep

- Have you considered the upkeep level of this room?
- How often will it require a good cleaning?
- Is it overwhelmed with dust catchers?
- Can it be cleaned easily?

Make this assessment for each room or area you intend to decorate. By the time you've finished, you'll know more details about that room than you ever thought could exist. But that's okay. The more you know, the better prepared you are to make the best choices.

In addition to assessing each of your rooms, your wish book can incorporate samples from your rooms and information about them. When creating your room-by-room wish book, you may want to:

- Include existing color schemes and any changes you anticipate. Visit the paint section of a local hardware store and pick up a few paint chips that match your current or projected colors.
- Include a small sample of the wallpaper you already have or the wallpaper you intend to use.
- Paste in some pictures of what you think you'd like the room to look like once you've finished decorating it. Make composites — different magazine pictures, your own artwork, anything that will begin to give you an idea of what you want. Include pictures of things you think you might like to use but aren't quite sure about yet.
- Note the textile colors currently in use, or what you'd like to use.

- Jot down overall room dimensions as well as accurate measurements of the space you intend to fill.
- Make a rough sketch of the room, including window and door openings or any other significant landmarks, such as a fireplace or built-in shelves.

The Item-by-Item Wish Book

A wish book might seem like a lot of effort when all you want is a table for your microwave oven, but many of the same guidelines apply even if you're seeking only a single object. So jot down these few things before you begin your hunting expedition:

- Why you want the particular item.
- How it's to be used in the room decor.
- Whether it will be a decorative or functional piece.
- Whether you are looking for something specific, such as a Wilton trivet, as opposed to just any trivet.
- The price you're willing to pay.
- A description (or picture) of what you'd really like if money and space were not considerations. Who knows? You could get lucky, and it never hurts to keep reminding yourself about the things you truly desire.
- Space requirements for the item.
- Room decorating schemes, including colors that have to be matched.
- Alternate uses for the item.
- Lists or pictures of things you've seen that could be modified to fit your needs. If you're looking for that great microwave table, for instance, an old sewing machine stand might be just the ticket.

Using Your Wish Book for Replacement Items

When you're shopping for replacement items, such as stemware, your wish book should include a picture of the set to which you're adding. That way you won't get confused when you find several different patterns of glass that closely resemble each other, as well being almost identical to those pieces of your grandmother's Cape Cod pattern you're trying to replace. Also, make a note of how many replacements you need, and when you buy one or two, change your count.

Cape Cod pressed glass was a good, sturdy, middle-of-the-road quality crystal when it was popular fifty or sixty years ago. Today its prices are still very reasonable, only a few dollars per glass in most areas of the United States. It may not look quite right alongside your fine china, but try using it with Currier and Ives dinnerware for a homey, Americana meal.

Using Your Wish Book

Half of the fun of shopping for antiques and collectibles is the wish process. Everyone who has ever set foot into a mall or show has had a wish or two, and those who are persistent enough to keep hunting will eventually see their wishes come true. The great thing about antiques and collectibles is that you don't have to buy the first thing you see for fear it's the only one of its kind, or the best deal you'll find. You can walk away, find something even more exciting, or make a better deal with the confidence that you can achieve your wish if you work hard enough. Granted, you'll have to be practical about it. Chances are you won't find the solid cherry

1840 bedroom suite for $600, but maybe a circa-1930 veneered waterfall style for $600 might look absolutely gorgeous in your bedroom. If that's the case, your wish has come true, but in a form you didn't anticipate.

Wish books help keep you organized, but as you hunt, and as you find yourself immersed more deeply into the world of antiques and collectibles, your wishes will change. You may find you love the waterfall bedroom suite so much that anything you desired before you bought it has faded completely from your mind. When this happens — and it will — your wish book will turn into an ever-evolving work-in-progress that reflects all you learn and see.

Keep Careful Records

Keep a separate record of all your transactions. Record all the pertinent information about the purchase, including date and place of purchase, amount paid, a receipt, and a photo of what you purchased. As your wishes or desires change, you might find yourself wanting to sell that waterfall bedroom suite and buy the solid cherry one you originally wanted. And it's nice to know the details of the original purchase in order to make a good sale. If you think you'll remember them, think again. If you're a onetime buyer, chances are you *will* recall the purchase price and all the finer details of the transaction, but if you're like thousands of buyers who catch the bug and keep on buying, all the buying trips and experiences will quickly start running into each other.

Finding Your Favorite Style

Style preference is one of those quirky things that differs from person to person. You may fall in love with a primitive flour bin and think the most wonderful thing about it is the rough shape it's in — warped boards, chipped paint, squeaky hinges. The primitive style may have a special appeal for you. The person shopping right behind you, though, might look at the same flour bin and think that it isn't even worth hauling to the curb for the trash collectors.

Webster defines *style* as "the way in which something is made or done," and the way the primitive flour bin was made suits you just fine. The styles you like are a matter of choice; there are no rules to dictate what you should or shouldn't like. Everything is fair game, but if you're not sure just what game you're after, there are several ways to discover your preferences.

First, go back to your wish book. Your own preference in style will stand out in those pages you put together, and it might surprise you to find that there is a common denominator in the things you've chosen to include. Do you see any similarities? Is all the furniture you've included oak? Perhaps all the glassware you've selected is actually pottery. Maybe the pieces you've included in your book are all very angular — cut with straight, clean lines and an overall no-nonsense appearance. Art Deco, perhaps. Or maybe you lean toward something more ornamental, something more Victorian.

Next, consult some references written by experts. You've heard that advice before, but if you're inexperienced, these books can be your best friends. They will acquaint you with a style and may even save you from overpaying if the asking price is miles away from the value indicated in the book.

Finally, browse. You've heard that before, too. Over and over. But browsing is the best way to get hands-on experience, and by browsing you probably begin to notice similarities in some of the objects you like. Certain things will inevitably catch your eye, and many others won't interest you at all. That shopper who hated your flour bin could be in the middle of purchasing a fine Queen Anne table with its slender and gracefully carved cabriole legs. You, however, have a definite bent toward the primitive style — something homemade and unrefined in craftsmanship, made to serve as a utility piece and not for show or display purposes. And you wouldn't have a Queen Anne table in your home if someone gave it to you.

Popular American Styles and Periods

The first American furniture was built shortly after the first colonists arrived. It was simple, often influenced by British design. Typical early American pieces included chairs, tables, chests, and chests of drawers. Historically, the following categories have been the most popular types of American furniture.

Colonial Furniture (1625–1776)

The name *colonial* is given to furniture that was built while America was still an English colony, and there really isn't one distinct design that can be called colonial. It's a catchall term for furniture used by the majority of settlers who lacked wealth and needed things that were plain and practical. But such furniture also often resembled fine pieces that were being produced in England at the time and were popular among the wealthy. Examples of British-influenced style include William and Mary, Queen Anne, and Chippendale.

- **William and Mary** (1700–1720) furniture is characterized by a long, slender, and graceful line and was among the first furniture made that actually catered to comfort. It is often tall — clocks, highboys, and tall-legged beds — and rich and dark in color. Walnut was the preferred wood. In comparison to styles that follow, William and Mary furniture is plain in design and ornamentation.

- **Queen Anne** (1720–1755) style is marked by its cabriole legs and other visually appealing curves. Surfaces are usually plain, and molding and ornamentation — often scalloped shells — were kept simple so not to detract from the beauty of the furniture's lines and curves. Walnut was the wood of choice in Queen Anne pieces, but curly maple, cherry, and mahogany were also used.

This William and Mary walnut dressing table is about 300 years old, but it still stands as a tribute to craftsmanship and elegance that is rarely ever reproduced today.

The high style and elegant line of Queen Anne furniture were as popular 250 years ago as they are today. Make sure, though, that before you decide to sit in a walnut chair, you check out its value first. In today's antiques market, some of the great old chairs might be worth more than your car. And if the fabric is original, all the better — the value might be closer to that of your house.

If it has wonderful ball-and-claw feet, or in the case of this 225-year-old mahogany chair, hairy-paw feet, it could be a Chippendale. Be careful when you think you've spotted an original, though. Those typical trademarks often postdated the style, and today one of the clever devices for selling a newer piece is to attach original ball-and-claw feet to it. Be mindful of this when you buy.

♦ **Chippendale** (1755–1790) style is marked by an abundance of finely carved ornamentation and the free use of curves. It is sturdy furniture characterized by ball-and-claw feet, and the wood of choice was almost always mahogany.

Federal Furniture (1776–1830s)

The name *federal* was given to furniture produced after the American Revolution. It deliberately lacked British influence, and in most cases it also lacks ornamentation, except for patriotic symbols, like eagles and stars, and pineapples, acanthus leaves, and lyres. Mahogany was a favorite wood for federal furniture, and it was often used in combination with tiger-striped maple or bird's-eye maple. Crotch mahogany was also popular.

It's hard to picture six guys with cigars hunched over this two-hundred-year-old federal card table, but in an entry hall under a beveled mirror and decked out with a fresh floral arrangement, this table would catch the eye of even the most avid poker player.

Victorian Furniture (1837–1901)

This furniture had its start in a plain, straight-lined style but, over time, transformed into something more visually appealing. With the advent of new tools and machinery, the late Victorian period was also marked by ornamentation in the form of gingerbread, curlicues, and fretwork. Some experts believe such ornamentation is excessive. Favored woods included walnut and pines stained to look like walnut. Mahogany, rosewood, maple, and cherry were also used. Metal furniture in the form of ice cream chairs and metal beds also appeared on the scene during the Victorian era, and it was during this time that marble became a popular option for tabletops.

Victorian furniture, such as this c. 1860 settee, was lovely to look at and definitely the finest furniture of its day, but this parlor piece simply wasn't comfortable for more than a few minutes at a time. You can almost imagine a finely starched gentleman courting a lady on this seat. But they would sit rigidly on the edge, hands folded neatly in their laps, backs straight, uncomfortable. For those with teenagers a' courting, a Victorian parlor settee like this one might be a good investment.

Victorian ice cream parlor furniture is aesthetically pleasing but uncomfortable for sitting. The idea was to lure customers into the shop with a quaint setting, then hurry them away with a hard wooden seat.

Art Nouveau Furniture (1890–1914)

This short-lived European style of furniture is marked by curving and swirling, often in the form of vines. It saw limited popularity in the United States and was seen less in furniture than in glassware and jewelry, both marked by the typical swirls and often displaying nude women or women with long, flowing hair.

Art Deco Furniture (1920–1940)

This modern style of furniture was the first to be produced entirely mechanically. Its lines are clean and straight, and it rarely has ornamentation.

Art Nouveau furniture, such as this c. 1900 chair, never really caught on in America as it did in Europe, particularly in France. The pieces that still survive today present the artistic, flowing lines that served as a counterpoint to the industrialized approach to manufacturing that took hold at the turn of the twentieth century.

Art Deco took America by storm and was a rebuttal to Art Nouveau's protest against industrialization. Pieces such as this c. 1920 chair are as angular and industrialized as Art Nouveau is flowing and artistic. Today, almost anything Deco is in high demand.

Primitive Furniture

This can come from any time period and features simple construction done with hand tools, incorporating native woods, such as pine, maple, and cherry. It lacks ornamentation and was meant to be useful, not attractive or comfortable. But today, primitives made well into the first few decades of the twentieth century are becoming favorites in many homes.

Shaker Furniture

Shaker furniture, like primitives, comes from different time periods, most notably the nineteenth century. It was produced by a communal religious sect founded in England in 1747, whose members danced on wooden floors as part of their religious worship and literally shook the building, hence the name *Shaker*. Anything ornate was believed to be an affront to God, so the Shaker religion dictated that anything Shaker-made be plain.

The furniture was made to be functional, but unlike the primitives it is highly refined and skilled in its craftsmanship. Its design is simple, basic, and straight, lacking all ornamentation.

There's a huge market for Shaker furniture, so if you buy Shaker, be sure to find out whether it's an original or a modern reproduction.

This primitive chair with its cane seat is close to a hundred years old. The man who made it probably sat in it every day for sixty or seventy years as he ate his meals. Wouldn't he be surprised to learn that the old piece of junk he knocked together in his barn is now worth more than his barn was when he built it?

The Shakers were masterful architects and innovators, and anything authentically Shaker is sturdy and functional.

DUMBWAITER

A tiered table placed beside the dinner table to hold serving plates, in lieu of a servant.

ECLECTIC STYLE

Drawn from various sources; heterogenous.

Old tobacco tins are some of the hottest collectibles on the market today. Good examples, such as these Edgeworth tins dating from the first third of the twentieth century, are great little storage bins, but a grouping of them can serve as a wonderful display, too.

Creating Your Own Style

Years ago no one would have been caught dead mixing and matching period pieces and different styles. Today whatever you like is perfectly fine, and no one cares that the circa-1880 china closet is sitting right next to a 1940s dumbwaiter. It simply doesn't matter. And one of the most important things about living comfortably with your collectibles is choosing what you like as well as something that's comfortable in your home.

Eclectic style is the newest antiques and collectibles trend, and it's catching on so well that it probably won't go away. Why? Most people have found that there are so many wonderful pieces from so many different styles that it's hard to choose just one style and stick to it. Even the most stringent antiques and collectibles shopper will get sidetracked from time to time and buy one item that was priced too low to pass up or was simply intriguing. And what if the small collection of Edgeworth tobacco tins he's been working on for a year doesn't really fit into his swinging 1960s bachelor pad? Does it make a difference? No — not as long as he's happy with it and it makes his living space a little more comfortable or enjoyable.

Buy What You Like

There's only one rule when it comes to buying antiques and collectibles for your home and that is to *buy what you like.* Don't let anyone convince you otherwise. The decorating rules that your mother or grandmother used twenty-five or fifty years ago no longer apply. If you'd like to see how those old rules worked, go find a few copies of any of the women's magazines in your library; try something from the 1930s to the 1950s. The homes depicted were in perfect order, with perfectly matching furniture and accessories. Color schemes were exact, matching and blending perfectly. Floral and other fabric patterns were not interchanged. Living room furniture came from the same set, with one sofa and one or two matching chairs. Wooden furniture was built in the same style or pattern, always in one room, and often throughout the house. Heaven forbid that you should mismatch your woods.

Mix and Match

Today, though, anything with visual appeal works. You can mix and match your florals, combine two or three different woods in one room, and even be so bold as to create a living room with furniture that doesn't come close to being from the same set, let alone the same era. And if you look in the currently popular women's magazines, you'll see that the styles are very different from what they were fifty years ago. Comfort is in, and it's coming in every form you can imagine. When you begin to think about decorating, then, be open-minded. Get away from the 1940s perfect look — unless that's the look you love, in which case you should definitely use the old magazines as your guide. Visualize an old wooden trunk sitting in front of your three-year-old mauve and blue sofa. Think about your brand-new big-screen television sitting on a 1930s end table. It all fits together in *your* own special way, and what always works best are the things that make you comfortable and happy.

Early tiles that are signed and dated by the artist may cost hundreds of dollars, but common household tiles like these vintage pieces can cost just a few dollars — often considerably less than their brand-new counterparts. Whether you mix them or match them, use them or display them, tiles make beautiful accents for the home.

CHECK OUT THOSE PRICE TAGS!

The big downside to shopping for antiques and collectibles is always what you have to pay. There's no getting around it. The most perfect armoire you've ever seen — the one that you've hunted for months and that'll be a perfect fit in your guest room — is priced about $500 more than you can afford, even after the discounts you've negotiated are applied. Should you grit your teeth, make the purchase anyway, and tell the kids you're really sorry, but you're cutting their school lunches back to every other day for the next couple of years or so? Or should you walk away, casting an occasional sad glance over your shoulder in the fleeting hope the dealer will take pity on you and lower the price to something reasonable before you're completely out of sight?

When you go antiques and collectibles shopping, you'll often feel much like the fisherman who comes back with the story about the one that got away. It was on the line, and it could have been his, but he just couldn't hang on to it. Sounds like the armoire story, doesn't it? It was on the line, and it could have been yours, but you just couldn't hang on to it — especially not when you realized you'd have to take the food out of your children's mouths to buy it. Experienced shoppers know there are always going to be treasures that get away for one reason or another — sometimes several in one shopping excursion. It's disappointing, but it's a fact of life. You probably can't afford everything you want.

For years, armoires like this c. 1850 primitive were not highly favored among antiques lovers because of their size. Today, though, these massive floor-standing closets have come into their own.

Moving On

Discipline is an important part of shopping. If you don't learn how to exercise it, you'll end up being someone who buys everything that strikes your fancy. If your house is the size of a warehouse, that's not a problem. And if your financial resources are unlimited, you don't have to worry about what your favorite pieces cost. Most people, however, have limited space and money to spend, and these two elements require that you exercise discipline.

Sometimes the deal you want just won't materialize no matter how hard you work at it. That jardiniere is twice the price you can afford and the dealer won't, or can't, offer a price that will make you both happy. What happens next — and it's something that happens to all antiques and collectibles shoppers — is that you'll walk away. You'll be forced to exercise some discipline because you have no other choice but to leave the jardiniere behind. Sadly, if it's the one you've been hunting for many months, walking away is tough.

When you walk away, don't think of it as a heartbreaking situation. Another jardiniere like the one you want will be out there, and you'll find it someday. At that time, you'll be in a better financial position, or the price will be something you can afford. So when you part company with that jardiniere of your dreams, don't look back. Just think of it as an opportunity to find something better, because you most likely will. Everyone who engages in a substantial amount of hunting and shopping learns to deal with the disappointment of not taking away everything they want. It's just part of the process.

chapter 5

Planning Your Purchases

i t's a lovely hutch, and it fits into your budget. But will it fit into your home? Is the size right? Will it overwhelm the space in which it will sit? Or, possibly, will it be dwarfed by its surroundings? Do you have a specific use in mind for it? Will it be hard to clean and take care of? There are a lot of things to think about when you are considering decorating or redecorating with antiques and collectibles, and a little forethought and preplanning can save you time, effort, and money down the road.

INVENTORY WHAT YOU HAVE

First things first. What do you have that you intend to keep, no matter what? Nothing? Everything?

Before you begin to plan what you'd like to purchase, it's wise to assess what you already have. Then you can come up with a mental image of what you anticipate adding to the room. Here are some questions to ask yourself when you're constructing your *toss it out* or *keep it* list.

- Is there any sentimental value attached to it? How much sentimental value, really?
- Does it have a practical function that will make it hard to duplicate?
- Is it a family piece or heirloom?
- Do you like it? Loathe it?
- Can you live without it?
- Will you miss it when it's gone?
- Will you subconsciously seek something else similar to it as a replacement?
- Will you be glad it's gone?

The answers to these questions will lead you to what should be a logical decision — to discard or keep the item in question. In many cases, the decision will be obvious. You've hated that piece-of-junk table from the moment you dragged it home, and you can't wait to replace it with something of much better quality. So, bye-bye table. You can heft it out to the curb and hope a scavenger will see it as a newfound treasure, or you can call a local charity to come pick it up. But what if that table has some senti-ment attached to it — it's ugly but it belonged to your great-grandmother? You may not like it, and you'd really prefer to get rid of it, but a nagging doubt is creeping in. The solution to this problem is simple. Don't get rid of it, or anything, when there's any doubt. Not even in the excitement of replacing it with something else, some-thing you really love. Wait a while. Make the decision in another month or two, because once it's gone, it's gone, and you probably won't be able to get it back. Or think of some other uses for it. Could it serve as a desk some-where? Maybe it would make a great extra storage surface in your kitchen. Do you need a worktable in the garage, or a table on which to do your arts and crafts?

There's another simple solution that could work, too: Give that table to a family member who would appreciate and cherish a fond remembrance of Great-Grandma.

Making Changes

So now that you've decided what goes, it's time to take a good look at what stays and how you intend to make changes to blend what you'll keep with what you'll buy. First, think about the changes you'd like to see.

One farmer's milk can might be another person's umbrella stand. Whether you paint it, stencil it, or leave it like it is, once you set it on the floor near your door you'll be amazed by the variety objects that will find a home there.

- ◆ Are they subtle? Do you intend to buy a few inconsequential items and blend them in with their surroundings, or do you hope to make a bold change such as starting with all new-to-you furniture?
- ◆ What's the reason behind your planned changes? More practical use? Better use of space? You're tired of what is already there?
- ◆ Do you have an idea what kinds of things you'd like to go where, or will you decide when you find it and fall in love with it?
- ◆ Do you need it or want it?

In a sense, this is where you'll start to become your own decorator. You'll be forced to make decisions professional decorators make every day, but your advantage will be that you are decorating for yourself, not someone else, and every choice you make can be something that pleases you. So, what if you want the old milk can sitting in the middle of the room to hold a few walking sticks or umbrellas? If you like the look, nothing is stopping you from that little bit of decorating whimsy. The change to your decor is solely yours, and the only thing stopping you — other than the obvious budget and space constraints — is your ability to visualize what you want.

Comfort versus Aesthetics

Aesthetic means "appreciative of the beautiful," but in terms of your own home, who is the person who should decide what beauty is? It's you, of course. You have to live there, and those collectibles will become a part of your everyday life, so the decision is all yours — no matter what the antiques guides tell you. You can do what you wish: Decorate any way you choose, mix and match, or stick with a particular style or pattern to design your own home in terms of what seems beautiful to you.

Trying to balance aesthetics with comfort has always been a big concern for shoppers, especially when they are hunting for pieces that will be incorporated into their daily lives. Should you buy something that's beautiful and not so comfortable, or go for comfort and skip the aesthetics? And how important is practicality?

If you intend to live with your collectibles instead of only collecting them for display purposes, you really should put comfort and practicality high on your priority list. That's not to say you can't have beauty, too, because you can. The first evaluation of anything you think you'd like to buy, however, should be the *stretch out in it and kick your feet up* factor — in plain terms, how comfortable it will be in your home and how practical to your lifestyle. A seventeenth-century French courtesan, Ninon de l'Enclos, once said, "That which is striking and beautiful is not always good; but that which is good is always beautiful."

Visualize!

Close your eyes for a moment. Think about your room as it is right now, then mentally remove a piece of furniture you intend to get rid of and replace it with one you think would look nice there. Keep your eyes closed and answer these questions:

- Does it fit into the space you intend for it?
- Does it fit into the overall scheme of the room?
- Does it look good?
- Does it look better than what it's replacing?

If you can answer yes to all four questions, it's time to place that item on your shopping list, or to drag it in from the garage if you've already bought it.

So when you've found a really nice mid-nineteenth-century sofa, ask yourself:

- Is it a piece that will be used frequently?
- If it's a piece that will be used only occasionally, will it be comfortable for a few hours use?
- Can you make yourself comfortable on it?
- Do you feel safe sitting on it — not afraid it will break?

Consider Clutter

Clutter is often associated with antiques, and the truth is, many collectors find themselves collecting clutter. They can't resist it, and there's always room for one or two more in the house, somewhere. Clutter is fine if you can manage it — keep it clean, dust on top of it, dust under it, dust around it, move it to dust behind it. But if you can't, your clutter will eventually turn into one great big dust bunny, and the aesthetic value you were trying to achieve will be buried under an inch-thick layer.

When you purchase any antique or collectible to be a part of your household, give its cleaning and care some consideration, because simple, basic maintenance will be required to keep your piece in its best condition. If you doubt that you'll be inclined to dust the prisms on a 150-year-old lamp every few weeks, consider a lamp without prisms. If the picture frame has too many ornaments to keep clean, consider one that's plain. When you make the investment, part of the responsibility is the care, but if your antiques and collectibles cease to be treasures and start to become clutter, it's time to evaluate how much time and effort you're willing to spend to keep them in their best and cleanest condition.

A late nineteenth-century oil lamp like this one is exceptional in its original condition, but cobwebs and dust are bound to collect on the prisms. If you're not fond of cleaning, choose something else.

Evaluate its practical use, too, if it's not an item intended for sitting:

- Is there enough space for ample storage?
- Is it durable? Will it stand up to frequent use?

After you've considered the elements that are essential to comfort and practicality in your home, take a second look at the piece in terms of its beauty. By now that beauty is growing on you. It happens all the time — love at second or third sight, or true love after you've lived with it for a while. You'll be amazed at how quickly something comfortable can change into something beautiful.

Everyone has a standard of aesthetics, and that's what makes the word of antiques and collectibles exciting: No two people have exactly the same standard. That variable standard will make your home one of a kind, however you choose to decorate it.

EMPIRE
Furniture made in France from the early nineteenth century until 1830. It was rigid, formal, and heavy — made less for comfort than for looks. Wood choices were dark, often stained or painted black, and fabrics were dark, too.

Consider an object's place in your home, as well as its appearance and condition, before you buy. This gorgeous 175-year-old Empire sofa is in perfect shape, but it's stiff and formal and not made for comfortable seating. Of course, if you don't care for long visits from your guests, this sofa might be a perfect addition to your home.

MORE CONSIDERATIONS

Now that you've been thinking for a while about what you would like to do in your home, it's time to start the real planning. You know you want a comfortable feel to the room you'll create, you've chosen some practical uses for the collectibles you'll purchase, and you've even come to terms with some of the changes you intend to make in your home. Most important, you've done some homework, you've browsed enough that you've become familiar with several things you'd like to buy, and you've learned the fine art of negotiation well enough to stand toe to toe with a dealer in heated debate.

You're getting close to the final steps now — buying and then living with your choices. But first, there are some pointed questions you must ask yourself about your space and how it will be used:

- ◆ Specifically, how will the room be used once it's furnished with collectibles?
- ◆ Will it be formal? Informal?
- ◆ How many people will use the room? Who are they?
- ◆ Do you need to have your rooms stay as they currently exist, or can a dining room be turned into a family room, a bedroom into a den?
- ◆ Do you want to stick with one overall style, or are you looking for a good mix of anything that appeals to you?
- ◆ What about reproductions — are you willing to use them, or would you prefer to decorate with only vintage pieces and antiques?

The process of decorating with collectibles can become pretty complex when you start weighing all the options available to you, but options are what make decorating and living with collectibles exciting because they are limitless. Following are a few more things you might wish to consider as you browse through your wish book and start to put the finishing touches on the wishing process.

Budgeting

A budget can be your best friend in the long run, if you create one and stick to it. Sure, shopping within its limitations can be difficult when what you want is out of your financial reach. Conversely, shopping within the preset limits can also be a great experience, especially when you've found the perfect item that fits your budget. Budget shopping can take much longer to accomplish, but if you enjoy the hunt as much as you do owning the object, then budget shopping shouldn't be a problem. It's just an opportunity to be responsible about your shopping.

Setting an antiques and collectibles shopping budget can be done in any of three ways. You can:

1. Set your budget according to how much you intend to spend on an entire room.

2. Set your budget according to how much you're willing to pay for a specific piece. This is where your wish book and all that browsing will help. You know you want an old Boston rocking chair, and because you've spent some time browsing and reading a few books, you have a pretty good idea what these are selling for in today's market. Budget the average amount you've seen being asked, or what the book tells is the current price, then stick to it.

3. Set your budget according to the dollar amount you're willing to spend on any given

---

Budgeting Tips

When you set a budget for a room, recall that:

- The costs of items vary greatly, so don't blow your budget on one or two things when it was your original intention to purchase six or seven.
- Apportioning your money is a great help. For example, you might apportion one half for major furniture, one fourth for lighting, one eighth for textiles such as rugs and curtains, and one eighth for knickknacks.

While cradles have had rockers for centuries, rockers weren't added to chairs until the late eighteenth century. Nana White rocked six babies in a Boston rocker like this one, starting in 1907 and continuing to her first great-granddaughter in 1980.

shopping trip. You have $100 in your pocket, therefore you will spend $100. This method of setting your budget can:

- **Make you more value conscious,** since you know that after one purchase, you'll have less money to spend.
- **Encourage you to comparison shop.** Sure, you have $100, and it only costs $75. But what if you browse a little more and find it for $50? You'd end up with $50 left over instead of $25. Right?
- **Teach you personal restraint.** If you take only $100 in cash with you and leave the credit and ATM cards at home, you can't go over your budget. And nothing teaches personal restraint better than the self-limiting experience of having only $100 when what you want costs $125.
- **Make you a better negotiator.** Dealers really don't fall for that "I know it costs $125 but all I have is $100" routine. However, when it costs $25 more than you have, you'll hone your negotiating skills pretty quickly if you really want to take it home with you.

In Irish pubs years ago, a patron would take a bottle of fine whiskey to his table and mark, with his signet ring, a line to which he would drink. When he'd poured out the whiskey to meet that line, he would, in theory, stop drinking, partly because of the cost of the fine whiskey, and partly in an attempt to stay reasonably sober. "I'll go this far and no farther" is what he would say, and that's what you'll have to say when you allot a certain dollar amount to spend per shopping trip, room, or item. You'll be faced with drawing that line and not stepping over it — partly because of the cost of the antiques and collectibles you want, and partly in the attempt to stay reasonable in your purchases.

One last word on budgets. Stick as close to it as you can, but do provide for that *I-just-couldn't-help-myself* occasion when you go over a bit. Normally, 15 to 20 percent is a safe amount to count on, but don't shop expecting to use it. Save it for an emergency or for a once-in-a-lifetime *I'll-die-if-I-don't-get-it* antique.

Making the Adjustment

There are several ways to adjust your budget to afford the things you want. The first is compromise. Do you want the armoire badly enough to forgo something else that might cost the $500 extra you'll have to pay to get the armoire? It's a hard choice, but one you'll be faced with from time to time if you make antiques and collectibles shopping a hobby. In other words, which thing do you want most? What will fit better into your home, your lifestyle? What is your priority?

If something you want is priced way beyond your means, the next thing to do is ask about a layaway plan. You won't get one at a show, but many shops and malls do offer them. Normally, you'll be required to leave a deposit of 20 percent or more, then make payments until the armoire is paid in full. Some malls, however, have a stipulation that merchandise not paid for within a certain number of days will be forfeited. Make sure you inquire about the layaway arrangements you establish, including the length of those terms and how long they can be extended. Get everything in writing, too.

Another way to adjust your financial situation so that you can buy the armoire is to sell something you already own, or trade it. Dealers are always open to making other deals, and if you have a couple of dozen old fishing rods left over from your grandfather just gathering dust in the garage, maybe you can throw several in to your offer to reduce the cost of the armoire?

One dedicated fishing lure collector had his eye on a particular lure, but it was well out of his price range. His personal collection consisted of hundreds of old lures and assorted fishing collectibles, many of which were common, not particularly expensive, and quite salable to beginning collectors. He worked out a deal to trade several of his items for the one lure he wanted, and everyone was happy: The dealer received new merchandise that would be easy to sell, and the collector went home with his coveted lure.

And if trading doesn't work, remember that there are always dealers looking for collectibles to buy. Take a picture of those fishing rods to a show or antiques flea market and ask around. Have the rods handy for inspection, in your car if you can. If you're selling a smaller object, just take it with you. Remember the old saying *Out of sight, out of mind?* Dealers are much more likely to make a purchase from you if what you're offering to sell them is within their sight at the time of the offer.

Architectural Changes

The object of this book is not to help you create a whole new house or interior for your collectibles, but to teach you to incorporate your collectibles into your existing home. Experts might tell you that certain features should be addressed. Perhaps your windows could be updated, your drapes and curtains tossed in favor of new window treatments that better resemble something vintage or allow in more light. Maybe a wall or two can be moved or eliminated to make your rooms larger. You might even hear you should get rid of your wall-to-wall carpeting and have hardwood floors laid, because they go so much better with antiques.

If you have the money, these changes are fine. Some people even go so far as to build their homes around their collections. But you don't have to move walls and rip out carpeting to achieve the comfortable living style you want from your collectibles. All you have to do is mix and mingle them with whatever's there now. So as you do your homework and talk to experts, don't be swayed by the argument that you must make architectural changes to get the most from your antiques, because you don't. What you buy will look great anywhere you put it.

Time Requirements

The progress you make in your decorating efforts will be largely dependent on two things:

1. Your finances.

2. Your time.

The limits to your finances will dictate how much you buy at any given time, a topic addressed in chapter 4 and earlier in this chapter under Budgeting. Your time, however, and the time it takes to create the comfortable home, room, or living space you truly want is something you may not have considered. It's a huge piece of the total process, though. What you intend to accomplish will not happen in a weekend or two. Most likely it will take months, if you're

Don't Go Overboard

No matter how you choose to look at it, an antiques and collectibles budget is an extravagance. You can put up some cheap shelving instead of buying a century-old armoire if money is your *only* consideration. But chances are you want more than just cheap shelves — otherwise you wouldn't be reading this book. So when you decide to buy, decorate with, and live with your collectibles, it's important to create a budget that won't compromise other areas of your life. Many people go overboard, especially when they're beginners. You don't have to do that, though, and if you can only afford to set aside a few dollars a week, the beauty of antiques and collectibles shopping is that you *can* work toward your dream even with only those few dollars at a time. Be reasonable in your budget and your first shopping endeavors. Those treasures you truly desire will be there next week, next month, and even next year. So pace yourself, and pace your wallet, too!

diligent, or a year or two if your time is limited. Are you prepared to put that much time into your endeavors? Are you realistic about projecting a completion date for your project?

If you're like most people, your shopping time is limited to a few hours on the weekends, and probably not every weekend. It will happen in bits and pieces — picking up a rug beater here and a cheese grater there. If you don't enjoy shopping or you have a rigid deadline for your project, now's the time to give the next steps of your process some serious thought.

Ask yourself one question here: Can you live with a work-in-progress for however long it takes to bring it to completion, or do you want it done tomorrow? If you think spending a year hunting will be great fun and filled with exciting opportunities, you're a good match for the project you have in mind. But if you truly expect to spend three hours at an antiques flea market on Saturday afternoon buying everything you want, do the decorating on Sunday, and have an open house to show off your accomplishments on Sunday night, your expectations are unrealistic. Your open-house guests will probably be disappointed by having nothing to toast but a work-in-progress or a host of odds and ends that don't reflect your personality and preferences.

Before you even think about shopping, give some thought to the amount of time you can invest, as well as to the time you'll need to make this project something more than a quick buying binge at an antiques mall. Sure, you can fill a shopping cart with kitchen collectibles in three hours, but are they the collectibles that you want to reflect your taste and personality, or merely the first things you laid eyes on?

Creating a comfortable living area from collectibles takes time — lots of time — and to do it right you must be willing to take the time necessary. This is an important point and one about which you should be fully aware before you undertake any shopping. Time estimates cannot be made, because there's no accurate way to predict your successes or failures each time you go out to shop. You may return with a bounty of goods, or one lowly spice tin to decorate a shelf. If you're happy with the single spice tin and look forward to your next expedition, time is irrelevant. If, however, you are irritated by your lack of productivity, it's time to rethink your decision to decorate with antiques and collectibles. Their purchase is rarely expedient, and more often then not it's inconvenient. It can be frustrating or a complete exercise in futility. So evaluate your lifestyle and personality. Is decorating and living with antiques and collectibles really what you want to do?

What about the Kids?

Kids are always a consideration when you shop for antiques and collectibles. Some experts will tell you to put off your shopping until the kids leave for college; others will tell you to take a firm hand with your kids and not allow them to touch your collectibles.

If you want to wait for eighteen or twenty years, the first piece of advice is great. Or if you intend to shop for collectibles and then spend every minute either making sure Junior isn't within an arm's length of grabbing something breakable or, worse yet, scolding him about touching the antiques, both pieces of advice will work. But consider this: Junior is a full-fledged member of your family, and he should have the luxury of living comfortably around your collectibles, too.

So are you wondering right now how to do that, or if it can even be accomplished? Sure it can, with some effort.

- **Purchase nonbreakables.** This may eliminate you from the knickknack category, but with Junior to keep up with, who needs knickknacks to dust?
- **Don't invest tons of money.** Stick to the less expensive collectibles — ones that won't break your heart if Junior manages to scratch them or finds a way to add his own lavish Crayon decoration.
- **Always, always buy for safety.** No sharp edges, nothing protruding. Check and double check to make sure there are no detachable parts that can be harmful. When you're shopping, do keep Junior in mind. Don't make the mistake of buying it, lugging it home, and *then* thinking about how Junior will deal with it. Make that determination at the beginning.
- **Buy Junior a few of his own collectibles.** Ownership is one of the best ways to teach responsibility, so teach Junior to take care of his collectibles. Explain why they are not just everyday playthings. You can start when he's quite young — four or five.
- **Share responsibility.** When Junior proves he can be responsible with his own collectibles, teach him how to take responsibility for your collectibles, too. Make dusting them his weekly chore. Allow him to arrange and rearrange drawer contents. Ask him to assist in deciding where to place the item.

A toy truck or an animated coin bank might be the perfect way to introduce a child to the wonders of collecting. Play together with the toy, explaining all the while why it's special and must be handled gently. (Note: Vintage toys should be carefully inspected for sharp edges and potential choking hazards before being given to a child.)

Finding a Home for Your Treasures

Some rooms are well used, others are ignored. Perhaps the family room is the hub of your family's existence, but the dining room is never used unless company comes for dinner. The same goes for furniture and other items in your rooms. The old recliner in the corner may see action every day, but the straight-back wing chair will go for weeks before anybody but the cat sits on it. Every person, or family, develops habits in their living space, and these habits must be considered when you begin to bring collectibles into your home and use them. Do you want to put breakable knickknacks in the room in which your family always gathers, or would they look better and have better odds at surviving somewhere else—perhaps a room used only when guests come for a visit?

Do factor wear and tear into your decisions. Consider the placement of your collectibles and how they'll be used, or disturbed, in the normal course of a day, then ask yourself how they'll stand up to the wear and tear to which they'll be subjected. Will the antique quilt last when it's thrown over the back of the sofa in the family room and dragged down to cover up anyone who's cold? Or would the table holding Grandma's antique china cups and saucers be better placed in an out-of-the-way corner than sitting boldly in the middle of the room for anyone to bump?

Some items have their natural place in the center of a family's activities, but many don't. Consider your choices before you make any decisions on their placement.

Your child can live comfortably with collectibles, too, but it's up to you to define how that living will take place.

- What will you allow? Sitting, eating, drinking on the furniture? Jumping up and down? Set limits that are comfortable to you.
- Are you prepared to deal with damage if it occurs? If you live in fear of damage, rethink the collectibles to which Junior has access.

- Do you have the patience to teach and reteach the way you want Junior to behave around your collectibles? The more he knows, the more responsible he will become.

Junior doesn't have to be a problem, and it's really unfair to assume that Junior and collectibles won't mix without giving it a try. It's all a matter of priorities, and teaching him how to treat your collectibles should be at the top of that list. Certainly, though, if something does have great sentimental or financial value, tuck it away for a while. After all, kids will be kids, and even the best little boy will have a less-than-best day from time to time. And you don't want a disaster to happen that could have been prevented with a few simple precautions.

Don't Forget the Cats and Dogs

While you're at it, give your pets some thought, too. They could have a bearing on what you choose. Cats love soft, comfy fabrics, and if you've ever owned a cat you'll know just how hard it is to keep her from sleeping wherever she wants. If your cat has claws, you may wish to avoid items with a fabric covering: Cats and vintage fabrics often don't mix. Silks and other soft and shiny materials rip easily, and bulkier textured materials snag. And there's the cost. Good vintage textiles, still intact, are pretty expensive — probably too expensive for Kitty to use as a comforter. But Kitty doesn't know this, and the minute you introduce something new into her environment — a couch with fabric seat covers, an old pillow, a quilt — she'll have to inspect it and eventually sleep on it, because that's just what cats do. So think about the cat factor while you're shopping. If you don't mind a little feline fur, or a snag or two doesn't bother you, go for the fabrics. Otherwise, make a different choice.

Dogs, on the other hand, have a completely different set of rules for something new or different in the house. Most of them don't care what comes and goes. But if you happen to own a rather aggressive or dominant male, he may claim some of those new items. It's a fact of a male dog's life. He's territorial, and he wants to own as much territory as he can. This is especially true if the furniture's previous owner has owned a dog, and your dog can smell traces of that pooch on the pieces you're bringing into the house. Female dogs aren't territorial and won't stake their claim, but male dogs will, so check with your vet or pet store for a product that will either mask the other dog's odor or smell so offensive to your own pet that it'll keep him away from everything you've bought. Such concoctions are available, and a good spritz or two usually won't harm your collectible.

chapter 6

Going Shopping

a t last, the moment you've been waiting for. All your hard work and studying to this point are about to be put to use. Your wish book will soon become a reality book, and your visions a material part of your home. Here are a few last-minute tips before your shopping experience begins:

- ◆ **Don't overlook anything in terms of its decorating potential.** You might be pleasantly surprised by the way it will fit into your home and decorating scheme.
- ◆ **Don't mix your shopping expeditions.** If you intend to look for kitchen items, stick to that and don't worry about those bathroom collectibles. There will be time for them later. When you concentrate on a specific area of shopping or item you'd like to find, that single focus will help you see those items that you might have otherwise missed. Many collectors who set out with a certain goal — to find a spoon rack, for example — are amazed at the number of spoon racks that will turn up in their hunt when they've never really seen a spoon rack before. But then they haven't been looking for spoon racks, and those racks were probably in plain sight all along for anyone focused on finding them.

- **Don't limit your experience.** Just because your goal for the day is to load up on kitchen utensils, that doesn't mean those utensils are all you should look at — or buy, for that matter. You can keep a specific focus and still look around, so let your eyes wander a bit. If you've planned to buy a mantel clock at some point in the future and you discover the perfect one at an unbelievable price, buy it.

- **Allow yourself plenty of time.** Do some real hands-on shopping. Study anything carefully if you think you might buy it. Look for signs of aging, maker's marks, or other means by which to identify the piece. Try to find cracks or chips or obvious signs that the item has been repaired. Make sure it sits level and doesn't rock, isn't warped, and doesn't have another flaw or defect that could keep it from being everything you want. Stretch out in it, sit up straight in it, open and shut the drawers and doors, lift the lid, kick the tires if it has tires. In other words, take your time with the piece and get to know it. Once you buy it, you may have to live with it for years to come.

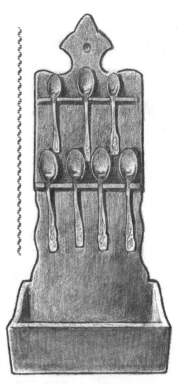

Spoon racks are typically made to display souvenir spoons, but this one-hundred-year-old version displays baby and toddler spoons that Nana White used to feed her children beginning in 1907 and continuing through 1925. The same spoons were used for her grandchildren and great-grandchildren, too.

Grandpa White's old Seth Thomas has dutifully chimed the hour and half-hour for nearly seventy years. When you decide to buy one like it, make sure it has a winding key that fits and that the clock is operational; otherwise your mantel clock will become a mantel knickknack.

Take-Alongs

A few basic supplies will help your shopping experience in ways you've probably never imagined. And you don't have to pack an extra bag to haul them along. Everything you need will fit into your pocket.

- **A good magnifying glass.** Any kind will do, so long as it is strong enough to give you a good, close look.
- **A tape measure.** Don't buy anything large without first knowing its dimensions.
- **A flashlight.** Many shows and shops are dark, and you want to get a good look at anything you're considering.
- **Pen and paper.** Taking notes along the way can often help you make good decisions. When you find something you might consider buying, jot down a quick list of its pros and cons, its asking price, and the price you've negotiated with the dealer. Don't forget to make note of the booth's location. You'd be surprised how often you think you'll remember exactly where it is, but after a long day visiting dozens of booths and browsing dozens of aisles, everything begins to look alike.

You don't need to be Sherlock Holmes to do some antiques sleuthing, but a few of these basic tools can be as valuable as Dr. Watson's assistance.

Take a Spouse

The best friend you can take shopping is probably your spouse, since that's the person with whom you share your living space. Granted, many spouses do not have the same passion for decorating that you do. Some lack a true appreciation for the vintage pieces you'd like to put in your home, while others simply don't care about the whole process. Still, it's always a good idea to extend your first invitation to the person who will be living with those collectibles, too. Include him in the process, or at least give him the opportunity to be included. Show him your wish book before you buy anything and ask if he has any ideas, wishes, or suggestions of his own. Call on his expertise: If he's a great carpenter, tell him you need his opinion on a piece of wooden furniture you might buy. Then, by all means, make his opinion count. Take his advice if he offers it. And remember, a little involvement in the process — no matter how little — is the beginning of an interest.

Not all couples who shop together share the same level of enthusiasm about antiques and collectibles, but when you've observed human nature for a while — especially among the couples who do shop together — you see threads of a common interest. Yes, hunting for antiques and collectibles sometimes does become a mutual interest. Sure, he may not like the dainty knick-knack collectibles you do, but then you probably don't have the interest in hand tools he has. But it evens out, and there can be great fun in something that turns into a joint hobby or leisure time activity you both enjoy.

Granted, you may occasionally see a wife who has insisted her husband come along whether he likes it or not; he's merely walking down the aisle behind her, carrying the packages, looking neither right nor left at anything on display. If this sounds familiar, consider these tips to get your uninvolved spouse involved in your shopping:

- **Start slow.** Try an hour or two for starters, and don't shop in a venue that is so jammed with people that the whole experience is an exercise in frustration. You want him to see the collectibles and get a feel for them, but if the crowd is suffocating, this won't happen, so pick your spot wisely — a mall or shop that's rarely too crowded.

Coffee grinders are collectibles unto themselves. Older models, such as this wall-mounted late nineteenth-century example, and similar-aged free-standing models, command a pretty high price.

- **Involve him at the browsing stage.** Explain what you'd like to eventually buy, and why. Show him examples. Let him get a feel for the prices. This will give him a better appreciation for what will happen when the shopping does take place.
- **Plan your trip around another activity.** Shop or browse for a couple of hours, then take him to lunch or a movie.
- **Always make sure at least half of the expedition is spent hunting and looking at collectibles he will enjoy:** men's tools, old toys, military memorabilia, hunting and fishing collectibles, sports collectibles, coffee grinders. Every show and mall will have as many displays that appeal to men as women, so even if you don't like looking at the guy stuff, do it anyway. Maybe he'll be more enthusiastic about going with you next time if he knows there's something of interest in it for him.
- **Let him make half of the decisions.** After you've become familiar with several shopping venues, let him make half of the decisions about the ones to which he'd like to return.
- **Let him buy a few items that will make him comfortable in his home.** They may not top the list in your wish book, or fit into the decorating scheme you've planned, but he has a right to have some wish book items of his own.
- **Reverse all this advice if you're the husband who has to drag his wife along to shop for collectibles.** There are women who don't have the true appreciation for collectibles their husbands do, so spend a little extra time browsing the girl stuff to convince her it's not such a bad experience after all.

Take a Friend

Who says you have to shop with a spouse? Shopping with a friend can be great fun, too, especially if that friend shares your love for antiques and collectibles. Of course, shopping alone can be rewarding and often less distracting, just getting away from everything and everyone for a while. In fact, some people prefer to shop alone and plan their schedules accordingly. It's not a bad idea, especially if you're caught up in a hectic lifestyle and a little solitary time comes at a high premium.

But it never hurts to have a second opinion just in case you've overlooked some tiny crack or chip, and that's where a friend will come in handy. She'll find the flaw you missed and be the moral support you need when you can't quite make up your mind and need another point of view. She'll also act as the devil's advocate when your decision can go either way, and be brutally honest when you think something will look great in your home but it's really an eyesore that will make everyone talk about your bad judgment behind your back.

So invite a friend whose opinion you respect — just make sure she has the endurance for a whole day of antiques browsing. Let her know what you're looking for, and let her in on your budgeted price range. Give her a peek at your wish book, too, and maybe she'll come up with a few ideas you haven't thought of. Try your best to keep an open mind, and be receptive to her suggestions. Then treat her to lunch in the quaint little café in the antiques mall's basement. After all, you're dragging her along on your adventure, expecting a lot from her in advice, time, and support; that surely merits a chef's salad or chicken salad croissant, don't you think?

CHECK WHAT YOU BUY

Unless you're an expert, it's difficult to know exactly what you're getting. It looks good, and to your eyes it seems old. But you're at a disadvantage if you don't know. You can use the magnifying glass and flashlight you're toting, but what good will they do if you don't know what you're looking for?

Beginners can make good deals, and there are ways to overcome the obvious disadvantages. Most generally, observation is the best weapon you have. A few little insider tips, though, can help you discover some of the subtleties of age and condition, and make it appear to the dealer that you know more than you do.

Changed versus Original

An unfortunate reality is that all too often, a collectible is altered significantly — and as a result loses most of its value. The highest appraisal value for any piece comes when it is in its original condition, and that means everything about it is original: grimy paint, cracked varnish, and even a century or two's buildup of dirt. And the patina (a thin coating or color change that results from age and various environmental factors such as sunlight, air, and cigarette or cigar smoke) must be original if you ever intend to sell the piece with an idea of receiving its maximum book value price. So if the original coat of ugly black paint is intact but covers up a beautiful piece of walnut underneath, the black paint will be much more valuable than the beautiful wood. Why? People who are willing to pay top dollar for an antique or collectible will do so only to acquire something in its original condition. Anything else simply does not hold its value.

A Closer Look at Wood

With a little effort, age is easily determined on wood pieces because:

Wood shrinks. When new wood is cut, it begins to lose moisture, and as that moisture decreases, the wood shrinks. Many woodworkers prefer to let the wood cure, or age, and reach its maximum shrinkage before working with it. In bygone days, however, this years-long process was something furniture and cabinetmakers couldn't afford. They cut and built almost immediately, allowing very little time for curing. Consequently, shrinkage occurred for years thereafter.

Denser woods such as oak, maple, and walnut show little shrinkage, but softer woods such as pine can shrink visibly. Look for shrinkage in areas in which a cheaper wood like pine was typically used, such as drawers or furniture backs — areas that wouldn't necessarily be seen. Shrinking in these areas can often be seen by the naked eye. Look for wood pulling away from the side, or seams that don't quite meet. Also, check the bottom of the runner on an old drawer. It should be worn smooth from continual use, but if it's rough, it's probably pretty new.

Look for shrinkage in lathe-turned legs (legs that are round and ornamented). Older legs won't be perfectly round due to shrinkage, but new ones will. And check inset panels, especially if the panel is stained or painted; a slight pulling away can be detected, and wood that hasn't been stained or painted revealed.

Lathe-turned legs add a touch of class to almost any piece of furniture. A good way to get a sense of a piece's age is to look at the legs. Legs that are perfectly shaped — more round than oval — suggest a newer piece. Legs that seem out of shape — more oval than round — show shrinkage typical of an older piece.

Tool marks are often detectable, especially in softer woods. The first place to look for tool marks is in areas that would have never been seen, such as the bottom or back of an object. Often you can find cut marks still existing, and if those marks were made by a handsaw, they will appear as straight lines that are not parallel or in exact proportion to each other. Check the dovetail joints in the drawers, too. Machine-cut dovetails are exact — each is identical to the others. Handmade dovetails, however, are inconsistent. No two are exactly alike. On older pieces, you'll often find score marks, too — marks cut into the wood to serve as a guide. And occasionally, if you're lucky, you might even find some measurements or ciphering on the underside of a drawer or in some other unseen place. Furniture makers often marked their instructions right on the piece.

Just because it has dovetails doesn't mean it's old. Specially designed routers and jigs help modern-day woodworkers produce dovetails quickly and with great precision. Handmade dovetails, on the other hand, aren't consistently symmetrical throughout a piece, and tool marks may be visible.

Wood wears away with use, and any place normal contact has been made over the course of years should show signs of use. Chair feet wear down after years of being dragged across a floor. Front stretchers — the bar that crosses between the front legs of a chair — wear away from feet being hooked over them. Wooden chair arms will become especially smooth; the finish may even be completely gone from continual use. So when you're thinking about buying a piece of wooden furniture, consider the normal use that should have occurred, then look for signs of wear that would logically happen during that use.

Wood discolors. It changes color the minute it's exposed to air. This process is more often seen on unfinished wood, but over time, stains and paints will discolor, too. And identical woods that have been exposed to the same condition will oxidize consistently with each other, but different woods will discolor differently. It may be solid oak throughout, but if one board has been replaced at a later time, its color will not match the rest of the wood.

Exposure to other environmental factors helps advance this color change, too. Called *patination,* this process is one of the most difficult things to reproduce or fake on wood items, because it comes from years of wear and exposure to dirt, body oils, smoke, and everything else that can affect its exterior condition. And this buildup has a logical order. When you're considering a wooden object, assess all the areas that would be subject to patination — wooden handles, armrests, drawer fronts, the area surrounding a drawer pull or knob — and be especially suspicious of areas that have patination variations you cannot explain. For example, if the desk has a lovely dark coloring, check an area that would have never been exposed to the elements that cause patination. If its color is also dark — something so close to the outside coloring it's hard to tell the difference — someone has probably added some kind of patination in the attempt to deceive, because that area should be lighter in color. That's a patination variation with no logical explanation, often the sign of a fake, reproduction, or come-lately work.

What about the Paint?

A two-hundred-year-old colonial highboy may hold an appraisal value of $100,000 in its original condition, but if the exterior has been stripped or refinished in any fashion, that value can drop by as much as 85 or 90 percent. And wouldn't you feel bad if you were the one who considered the highboy a work-in-progress and spent several months stripping it down to its wood? Sure, to your eye that walnut exterior might be much more beautiful than the old black paint, but in the long run, reducing the value by so much isn't worth the effort you put into it.

The Cost of Marriage

When two or more original furniture pieces of differing origin are assembled into one piece, this is called a marriage, and while these may be interesting pieces to own, they rarely retain much value. Bookcases or cubbyholes were common late additions to desks; one type of dresser was sometimes stacked on a lower piece to create a highboy effect. Often this was done in an attempt to make the best of two broken pieces, and it's not uncommon for antiques dealers to do the same and sell the result as an original. Married pieces often don't look right. Their dimensions are out of proportion with each other; their styles don't match, nor do their woods. Patination isn't even, and workmanship usually differs, too. Check dovetailing and other craftsmanship techniques.

Buying a married piece isn't bad, as long as you know what you are getting. Certainly, the price should reflect the fact that it's not an original. If you detect a marriage, expect a price substantially lower than something similar to what you might find in the book.

It looks great as a desk, but it's really a c. 1850 two-drawer table with a c. 1800 cubbyhole section nailed to the top.

So when you're shopping, how do you know what's original and what isn't? Unfortunately, given the popularity of antiques and collectibles, it's hard to know, unless you're an expert. Too many inexperienced dealers have yet to wise up to the fact that original is better, and they automatically strip all paint and refinish a piece to make it appear to be in perfect condition. What they don't realize is that a century or two ago, paint was considered high style.

Also, there's a trend among people who strip and refinish furniture for a living of buying old pieces and doing just that, without any knowledge of what the piece is or what its value could be in original condition. And conversely, because original paint on any wooden furniture is highly collectible these days, there's a deceptive trend among those who sell collectibles of applying paint that attempts to duplicate an old style. If the piece is advertised as refinished or newly painted when it's offered for sale, that's not a problem. You know what you're buying. Unfortunately, more often than not the intent is to make you believe you're buying something with a really old patina or paint job, and the dealer will not indicate otherwise.

Experts in furniture restoration are the best judges of old furniture's true paint condition, but if you don't have an expert handy when you're shopping, or if you're thinking about doing a little handiwork of your own, there are a few things to look for that can help you determine if the paint is old or new.

- **Check the color.** Does it just seem too vibrant? Old paint doesn't look new, no matter what you do to it. Ask yourself if the color is right for something that old. Paint used a century or two ago

PATINA
A thin coating or color change that results from age. Good, original patina enhances value. Destroying it decreases value.

Vintage high chairs are certainly more beautiful than most new ones, but infant safety wasn't a consideration 70 or 80 years ago. If you select a classic model like this for your child, evaluate its safety and devise a secure way to fasten baby in.

came in basic hues, and the pigments actually came from nature — muted reds and oranges, browns and blacks. If it's a delicate pink or sky blue, the paint isn't original.

◆ **Check for overspray or splatter marks.** Many people who try to replicate old paint actually use paint sprayers for an undercoat.

◆ **Old paint on any old piece wears evenly if the piece has a specific function,** such as a chair. Wear will be indicated in the areas where a body has repeatedly contacted that chair, so if the seat's paint is almost flawless but the spindles or back seem to have more wear than they should, be careful. Also, check the bottom. Painted chair bottoms should have no wear.

◆ **Age causes shrinkage, cracking, and peeling paint.** Primitives are popular pieces to alter because they have a rough look already, and many were painted after they were built as the only decoration or beautifying mark on an otherwise utilitarian piece. Paint on older primitives is often wearing away and rough because of the texture of the wood used in the piece — and in this class of furniture, this is a highly desirable condition that adds to the dollar value. So on unpainted primitives, many people attempt to create the illusion. What they can't create, though, is the authentic cracking and peeling that happens with age. The edges of old paint are rough, drawn up from chipping and shrinkage. Feel the edges of the paint in areas where it's chipping away or patches of it are missing. Use your magnifying glass, too. See if the paint can be easily flecked away or is adhering to the wood pretty well. If it's adhering, it's probably not too old.

- **Beware of cracking paint.** Yes, old paint *does* crack, and it can take on a wonderful antique look. But original cracked paint in good condition is very desirable and commands high prices, so it's often duplicated on wood pieces that weren't painted or whose paint isn't cracking. Once you've seen the wonderful patina of old cracking, you won't mistake it for anything new. But until you've found a piece you know has authentic cracking, look closely before you buy. New cracking applies smoothly and feels smooth to the touch when it dries. Granted, there are cracks that prevent the surface from being completely even, but they still feel smooth when you run your fingers over them. Old cracking has a rough texture. The paint was applied in an even coat and has cracked and contracted, clear evidence of age. Also, visible brush marks that weren't meant to be decorative or attractive are often seen in old cracking; new cracking, however, takes on a uniform look with an applied glaze that prevents the brush marks from showing through.
- **Look for dirt and dust within cracked paint.** Old cracking is hard to clean without damaging the paint, so it's likely you'll find a bit of dirt and dust within those cracks. New cracking won't have that patina.

Has It Been Stripped?

Many stripped pieces can be beautiful and will look great in your home, but you have the right to know if you're buying something that's had its original finish removed. And if you are, don't pay book value, because the piece will never again sell for its original worth.

There are several ways to find out if your piece has been stripped. First, look for visible signs of paint or other original or old coloring. Certainly you won't see them in the most obvious places, but a close look with a magnifying glass will reveal signs in carved areas, joints or seams, corners, or anywhere else with limited access that would be difficult to strip. Look under any facade pieces that might hang down, too, such as carved ornamentation used as trim. If the piece has had another finish, it can be detected somewhere.

Another way to know if the piece has been stripped is to observe the wood. Does it look too bleached out? Bleached-out wood is the mark of someone who doesn't know how to strip furniture, and in pieces where this has occurred, excessive sanding has usually been applied, causing the wood's texture to lose its natural grain. Also, is it sealed with something that's too shiny — polyurethane, perhaps?

People do many things to make wood look better, or at least better in their estimation. When you're evaluating, though, it's up to you to determine just how the wood has been treated. In the end, if you love it no

An Ugly Divorce

Married pieces are common, but so are those that have been divorced, or altered to make them into something they aren't. For example, a dealer who has only the top of a highboy may convert it into a lowboy. Or if she has only the lower piece of a highboy, she may convert it into a simple chest. As with a married piece, check to make sure everything matches, patination is even, and there are no apparent scars or marks of alteration where something else might have once belonged. Never pay book value for something that has been divorced. These pieces do not retain much value.

matter what form it takes — painted, stripped, refinished — the price is right, and there's a perfect spot for it in your home, there's nothing wrong with buying it. One of the great joys of collecting old things is that no matter what their condition, they can still be valued, practical, and comfortable additions to your living space.

A Look at Glass

Unlike wood, glass doesn't shrink. It doesn't show much, if any, patination; wear is often undetectable to the untrained eye. And any normal wear that occurs — tiny scratches on a glass surface that regularly comes into contact with a hard surface, such as a shelf — can be faked with a piece of sandpaper. That doesn't mean wear can't be detected and you're a sitting duck when it comes to glass objects. It just means that what you should know about older glass is completely different from what you've just learned about older wood.

Reproductions are more common in glassware than any other form of collectibles. In fact, several glass producers today pride themselves in creating reproductions. Many even use the same molds that were used a hundred years ago, just to achieve the same look. Added to this is the fact that some good fake glassware intended to deceive is currently coming from Mexico, and you have a market that requires a keen eye.

So how can you be sure you're not buying a fake or reproduction? First, check for wear. Turn that bottle over and look for fine scratching on the bottom. Can you see it? Try a magnifying glass. If the piece is old, it's there, and it doesn't matter if that glass object is a vase, oil lamp, or figurine. Glass that has had a long shelf life will have scratches.

Though it looks gorgeous, this 25-year-old, $25 Mexican-made reproduction bottle is popping up everywhere and is being sold as an authentic antique. It comes in gold and blue. Unscrupulous dealers may invent an antiques provenance to go along with it, so be careful.

Now run your thumbnail over it. The scratching should feel satiny fine. If it has a rough texture, one that's easily detectable, it may have been applied by sandpaper, which is what the fakers do. But under the magnifying glass, you'll see that the faked scratches take on a different appearance — much larger.

Another way to become familiar with the scratches is to go find a bowl you've used in your kitchen for a number of years. Any old bowl will do, as long as it's glass. Turn it over and look at the scratching on the bottom. Now, rub your thumbnail over it. It has a certain feel to it that will be similar to the scratching you'll feel on old glass collectibles. Next, find a new piece of glassware, one you've just bought or hasn't been used much. Rough up a place on the bottom with sandpaper then scrape your thumbnail over it. Do you feel how that texture differs from the first?

If you're still not sure about the scratches you're feeling, set the piece down and look for areas where the glass makes a heavier impact on the surface. Old glass bottoms were rarely even; there are visible high and low points. High points show the most wear — scratches. Low points may be perfectly clean. Use a piece of carbon paper or something else that will trace the high points. If you find scratching in the low areas as well as the high, you've got a piece that has been altered in an attempt to deceive you.

Suppose you're afraid that vase or expensive bottle you're considering could be one of those well-made fakes from Mexico. How can you tell for sure? Old bottles have tiny bubbles in them, but the bubbles were usually pretty scarce. Too many indicated a flaw that could result in breakage, so bottles with an abundance of bubbles were discarded. Those modern fakes, however, are loaded with bubbles. There may be as many as hundreds or thousands in one piece — a condition that would never have been acceptable in old glassware. Those bubbles may be attractive, but if you want authenticity, put that piece of glass back. If you don't mind a fake — and many people don't, because they can be lovely — don't pay the price of an original. Those Mexican fakes are worth only a few dollars.

Another way glass shows wear is through decomposition. It literally breaks down with age, especially if it has been in contact with water or soil for an extended period of time. Sometimes it flakes, and often it takes on an opalescent look. Also, staining is common, especially in bottles and other glassware that has been used for storage of foods or medicine. Signs of age do not necessarily affect the value of glassware adversely, if the piece is intact without chipping or cracks. In fact, many people prefer to collect pieces that show definite age. So if you see a gorgeous bottle that looks more like opal than glass, and you think it will be attractive in your window, don't be put off by its condition.

Beware of Irradiated Glass

Clear glass from the middle to late nineteenth century can actually turn a faint amethyst if it exposed to prolonged periods of sunlight over the years. This is highly desirable among many glass collectors, but be warned that the coloring is *very* faint. Tricksters today have found a way to irradiate these old glass pieces to take on an artificially deep amethyst color, and they tack on a high price tag because of that color. This method is used primarily in old bottles, and there's nothing wrong with buying an irradiated bottle if you know what it is. Just don't pay the book price — especially not for a piece identified as late nineteenth century — because irradiation decreases value. And true purple glassware from that era carries a huge price tag to reflect the rareness of the color. So ask the dealer if the piece has been irradiated. After you've seen a couple of pieces that have, however, you'll be able to detect them pretty easily.

A Word about Porcelain and Pottery

These collectibles are among the hardest to detect as reproductions or fakes, because the techniques used for hundreds of years to produce them are still in use today somewhere in the world. So it's wise to use a few simple guidelines when considering a piece of porcelain or pottery. Just remember that unless you're an expert, there are few ways to really tell what you're getting.

- Look for signs of wear — scratches or chips. Minor problems will not affect value, but major scratches and chips will. Look for wear on the bottom, too.
- Painting or decorations applied after the piece has been glazed will wear away, even though the original glaze can remain unaffected for hundreds of years.
- Look on the bottom for a maker's or country mark. New pieces often have the country of origin stamped on the bottom, and it's not uncommon for dealers to sand that out and dab a bit of glaze over it to hide the fact that the item is fairly new. If you spot a blob of glaze that doesn't look like it should be there, be cautious.

Don't avoid great pieces of pottery if you can't determine their authenticity. Do, however, be judicious in how much you spend for one if you're not sure about it, and if it hasn't been authenticated to the point that you're convinced it is what it's represented to be. These pieces can make wonderful additions to your home in either practical or aesthetic functions, but do take a good look before you buy.

Scrutinize the Metal

Like wood, metals offer many signs of wear to even the inexperienced buyer. Except for gold and platinum, they oxidize and patinate, and they also show signs of manufacturing technique, wear, and alteration.

First, look for the oxidation or patination, and apply some of the same standards as for wood:

- Metal objects made of more than one piece patinate at the same rate and same pattern on all exposed surfaces.
- Variations without a logical explanation can be a sign that false patination has occurred. Today it's not uncommon to induce the rusting process to make a new piece seem old. True rusting that's the result of a prolonged oxidation process is uneven and inconsistent. Induced or artificial rusting, however, appears evenly over an entire surface.
- When metals that usually patinate naturally to green or brown — such as copper, brass, or bronze — are artificially patinated, the result can be an ugly black tarnish. Be leery of black tarnish on items that should patinate to another color.
- Copper can be aged by sprinkling copper sulfate on its surface, then baking it. The patination looks real in color, but it bakes on in a spotty pattern and can be broken away. Real patination will not chip away.

Next, look for signs of manufacture. Handmade items, especially those of wrought iron and softer metals, will show marks of hammering. And every hammer mark should be deliberate, with a purpose, and the strokes should be unobtrusive. On finer pieces the hammer marks were often polished out on exterior surfaces and left intact on inner surfaces not intended to be seen. And in any case, any hammered dent was small and rounded, never the deep, round kind you'll see in modern fakes and reproductions. Those wishing to fake metal objects know the importance of hammer marks, but their hammering often becomes a surface decoration. It's as if they're trying to announce the fact that this is a hammered piece.

Also, look for signs of normal wear. If the object has feet, wear will show on those feet in the form of scratches or nicks. Metal will also wear away, so prominent areas might show smooth or worn spots where frequent use has occurred, such as in a boot scraper. And like glass, many metal objects are not perfectly flat on the bottom; they'll show the high-low pattern of wear.

In softer metals, such as silver, years of polishing will round the contours and sometimes even rub out a good bit of any engravings. If you find a piece of silver with nice sharp edges, chances are you're looking at something that's had little polishing. This in itself is not an indication that the piece is newer, because it could have been stored away for decades. But in bygone days, silver was used and then polished much more than it is today. When you find a piece with nice, soft contours, then, it's likely you're look-ing at something old. If those contours seem a little sharp or rough, however, the piece could be new.

Volumes have been written on fakes, reproductions, and wear and tear, and it's not realistic to think you know everything you need to know in order to protect yourself against someone who's bent on passing off that new chair as an old one. Even the experts get fooled from time to time. But a little caution and the wise use of your bud-geted dollars will go a long way in your purchases. And after all, there's no rule that says you can't live happily or comfortably with a reproduction, is there? (For more information on identifying and pricing antiques and collectibles, see page 205.)

BUYING WITH A VISION

Many people look at the antiques and collectibles they buy as a project. They plunk down their money with the idea of taking a treasure home to strip and refinish, fill in the nicks and dings and touch up the paint, remove the attached mirror, cut the legs down a few inches, stencil and tole-paint. Whatever the plan, too many collectibles become something they weren't intended to be in the hands of people who have a different vision for them than that of their creators. And that's okay if you can carry out your plans, but it's easy to become one of those people who buy with an abundance of enthusiasm for what those collectibles can become, only to find that their plans never make it past the planning stage.

There's a perennial debate about whether pieces should be restored and refinished, and some things you buy will absolutely require work. If you buy a piece for the sake of having a project, or because it's the best you can afford or its price is so incredibly good you can't pass it up, that's fine. Fixer-uppers exist, and they definitely need someone to fix them up. Just remember that in many cases, your efforts will greatly reduce the value of the piece. If it's already in bad shape, though, that doesn't matter. And in some cases, a little tender loving care may actually turn something worthless into something that does have value.

When you buy that fixer-upper, however, don't just roll up your sleeves and get to work on it. Read a few books to learn what you're doing. Decide if you want to

TOLE-PAINT
A highly decorative, folk-art painting style.

try an authentic restoration or if you'd prefer to just create something that looks good enough to you. And by all means, if you lug it home and later discover you have an important piece — something potentially of great value or historic significance, don't touch it! Call a conservator. You can find one through a local museum or your historical society, and let her advise you about how to proceed. Most often that great find won't be so great in the eyes of a professional conservator or appraiser, but occasionally a rare piece does surface, and you really don't want to be the one to botch it. So play it safe. Find an expert.

Love It Just as It Is

Perhaps the simplest way to save yourself from the *to-fix-or-not-to-fix* dilemma is to love a piece as it is. Many experts will tell you to buy the very best condition you can afford. If you heed that advice, chances are you'll take home a piece that can exist in your home just the way you bought it. You may even be investing in something with the potential to appreciate over the years.

Sure, you can clean it up a little. Dust if off, maybe add a light coat of oil if the wood or leather is dry. Clean three inches of clay out of the bottom. Otherwise learn to accept the condition it's in; eventually, its little eccentricities will grow on you. And if it's in perfect condition to begin with, so much the better.

Keep in mind that when you buy it and later decide to make it a project, time, effort, and ability are all called into play. If you lack any of these, the table you intended to put to use immediately could end up months or years away from the service you need today.

Going Room by Room

as you know by now, there's only one rule to keep in mind when you begin your shopping: *You don't have to follow the rules.* You can buy whatever strikes your fancy and will fit comfortably into your home. You don't have to be traditional, either. Just because custom dictates that you put the rug on the floor doesn't mean it can't make a lovely wall hanging. And who says you can't use an old library table in place of a desk? So get your imagination in gear and visualize everything that catches your eye in terms of its decorating possibilities in your home.

KITCHEN/DINING ROOM

One of the great trends among collectibles enthusiasts today is outfitting a kitchen with odds and ends from the past. At flea markets, the booths specializing in kitchenwares are among the most popular. In antiques malls, older kitchen items have also become hot commodities simply because people are discovering that what was made fifty or sixty years ago is so often more pleasing and better functioning than almost anything made today. Older utensils are sturdier, pots and pans heavier, dinnerware and flatware more durable; the quality of the vintage kitchen cannot be denied. Added to this is the idea that a vintage kitchen also carries with it great sentimental appeal. Warm family memories have always been made in kitchens . . . bread baking in the oven, bacon frying on the griddle, sugar cookies still warm on the cookie sheet. Can you think of anything more nostalgic than cooking chicken and noodles just like your grandma made in a pot like the one she used?

Utensils

Cooking utensils are important if you like to cook, and for a relatively low price you can convert your utensil drawer into one that has vintage appeal as well as good quality. There are a few things to consider when you begin to buy, however:

- ◆ **Do your utensils need to match?** If so, you may want to consider hunting for matching pieces or buying a complete set to begin with. The biggest advantage to matching sets is aesthetic: They simply look good. The price is a disadvantage, though, because intact matched sets usually cost several times more than the individual pieces sold separately. Called orphans, these separate utensils are cheap. If you don't mind having a mismatched set, or hunting until you find a complete set, buying orphans is the way to go.
- ◆ **What utensils are you likely to use most often?** Put these at the top of your shopping list, followed by the ones that will find occasional use. Next,

ORPHANS
Individual pieces once belonging to a set that are selling as single or separate units.

consider this: If you've never used a rolling pin, do you really need one? Utensil drawers can become junk drawers pretty quickly, so buy only what you use. Otherwise you'll find yourself with a drawerful of unused gadgets that do nothing but take up precious space.

After you've given some thought to what you'd like to put in your utensil drawer, think about the condition of the items you'll purchase. Old kitchen utensils are rarely in perfect condition; they've been used and often abused, just like the ones you own right now. Vintage spoon handles may be a bit bent, for instance, or their silver plating could be worn in spots. These things won't matter if function is your primary concern. When you decide to make a purchase, however, there are several things you should check, and avoid:

- **Rough edges and nicks.** Don't trust your eyes to find them. Run your finger over all edges and surfaces.
- **Rough spots on handles, and handles that jiggle or are not attached securely.** The best handle to hold is smooth and secure.
- **Paint that is not worn away, but chipping.** Painted wooden handles were especially popular before World War II, a time when lead was not considered a health risk, and they may be painted with a lead-based paint. Avoid all old utensils with chipping paint.
- **Parts that bend but really shouldn't.** For example, a small child can bend a new spoon, but older spoons are difficult to bend even for adults. So if it bends easily, don't buy it.

Berry spoons are beautiful and functional; they are for me one of the greatest inventions known to mankind. Handles and edges should be smooth, not rough.

Let's take a look at some of those utensils you might use — both the common ones and those you may have never have considered.

Spoons. Spoons are always a necessity in a kitchen, and everyone uses them. They stir gravy, serve applesauce, scrape cake batter; you eat homemade chili off a spoon, taste bubbling spaghetti sauce from a spoon, and measure out sugar and cinnamon with a spoon. Anyone who spends much time in the kitchen has a favorite spoon or two tucked away in the utensil drawer ready for use. There's probably nothing wrong with the spoons you're using right now, but think about some of the advantages of older spoons: They're heavier, they don't usually bend, and they don't have plastic or rubber components that melt at high temperatures. Then ask yourself: When was the last time you melted part of your spoon into a pan of boiling fudge?

One of the best buys you can make is a berry spoon. It's an uncommon utensil, and you probably won't find one in a new set of flatware, but once you've latched on to an older berry spoon it will quickly become a favorite. A berry spoon is a serving spoon with a longer, deeper, wider bowl designed to scoop up berries in a single layer so not to damage them. Find one and you'll how great it is for stirring and, particularly, for serving.

Old wooden spoons are great, too, but be cautious before you fall in love with one. They can come with pretty high price tags, especially when they were handmade or predate the twentieth century. Much lower prices — usually around a few dollars — indicate a wooden spoon has been around for a while, but not more than several decades. Still, when you consider how many pots of stew it stirred, a few dollars might not be a bad price for something so well seasoned.

Vintage Measuring Spoons and Graduated Cups. These items are wonderful finds. Separately, they're most often sold at a reasonable price. Finding an intact set is rare, however, and the high price that comes with it reflects that rarity. Still, older examples are durable and often worth the price you'll pay. And if you don't mind the orphans, a few mismatched pieces for your utensil drawer will do the trick at a dirt-cheap price.

Old Knives. Old knives are great, too, but they come with their own set of warnings. First, check the blade carefully for nicks. Then pay particular attention to the thickness of the metal blade. Each time a knife is sharpened, it loses metal; over a period of years, a knife blade can actually become too thin to use and even become breakable.

Spatulas, Ladles, Gravy Ladles, and Other Serving Pieces. These are some of the most popular vintage kitchen items on the market today, and for many of the same reasons people are buying spoons, knives, and anything else associated with the kitchen. They're durable, they don't have plastic parts, and they won't bend under ordinary use. What more can you expect from something designed to serve food?

Nana White's kitchen utensils are still used every day. The ladles date from the 1930s and the spatula from the 1920s, and they're worth every bit of the few cents she paid for them way back when.

Ice Cream Scoops. Ice cream scoops — the old-fashioned one-piece, soda-fountain kind — are such a hot collectibles commodity that their hefty prices may surprise you a bit. Still, they're among the best utensils you can add to your drawer, and the price you'll pay will, over the course of your ice-cream-eating years, be worth it. Some come with a paddle-shaped scoop, others with a bowl-shaped, but regardless of the scoop shape, a vintage

Second only to a berry spoon in my kitchen, this one-piece Roldip ice cream scoop has dipped more times in its sixty years than anybody can count, and it is bound to keep on dipping . . . and dipping . . . and dipping!

ROLDIP

The Roll Dipper, or Roldip, was one of the first commercial ice cream scoops. The Zeroll Company — developer of the Roldip (now of Fort Pierce, Florida) — today is still known for its innovative scoop designs.

model will never fail you. It has the potential to last decades or even centuries. Over a lifetime, it will stand up to its duty well and serve far more ice cream than you'll be able to eat. In other words, if you find one, buy it!

Rolling Pins. Rolling pins can be a little tricky to buy. They're a separate collectible unto themselves, and also a favorite among collectors who specialize in glass items such as bottles, because early glass rolling-pin manufacturing techniques were much the same as for bottles. The earliest examples, some more than two hundred years old, are highly desirable and expensive — from hundreds to thousands of dollars. Later rolling pins were handmade from a solid piece of wood and carved as a single unit with no moving parts. These have a high value, too, and can sell for hundreds of dollars. Wooden rolling pins made from the early to the mid-twentieth century came with moving parts — the roller and handle units are separate — and aren't as collectible as the earlier ones. Consequently, they can still be found at reasonable prices.

When you find a rolling pin you like, check for these things:

- ◆ **Weight.** You don't want a pin so light that you have to put more muscle into the rolling than should be necessary, but you do want one that isn't so heavy it's a burden to use.
- ◆ **Smooth rolling action.**
- ◆ **No dings or dents on the roller.**
- ◆ **Easy handle grip.** If you use a rolling pin frequently, you definitely want to make sure that it feels good in your hand.

One warning about rolling pins: There are a lot of reproductions and misrepresentations out there. Brand-

new glass pins are being made to look like the old blown-glass models. Popular reproduction colors are cobalt blue and light pink. They are actually very pretty, and there's nothing wrong with buying one if you know what it is, but if you're not an expert you can be fooled pretty easily. Do your homework. Also, look for signs of legitimate wear. Rolling pins were made to be used, and the old ones definitely show the appropriate signs.

Handheld Potato Mashers. Handheld potato mashers may be one of the best things to come along since the electric mixer, and they're not just for potatoes anymore. How many times do you find yourself trying to mash stray lumps with a spoon? Do you get frustrated mixing the eggs, mayonnaise, mustard, onion, and other ingredients for egg salad with a fork? An old potato masher is a great little fix-it utensil for many tasks. Once you add one to your utensil drawer, you'll probably find some uses for it that no one else has thought of yet.

Handheld Crank-the-Handle Mixers. Handheld crank-the-handle mixers are another great buy. Remember them — the ones that actually did the job without electricity? They're wonderful little gadgets for mixing a small amount of food without dragging out and plugging in the portable mixer or revving up the old stationary model. They're also a testament to the idea that simpler can be better.

A utensil of many uses, this potato masher from the 1940s isn't picky. It will mash anything that needs mashing, and its use is therapeutic, too. A few good minutes of mashing are guaranteed to relieve all kinds of frustrations.

Pots and Pans

Older pots and pans are often an acquired taste. They can be found in metals ranging from silver plate to aluminum, copper, and iron, and because more metal was used in the production of older pots than is used today, they're often substantially heavier than anything now on the market. Quite honestly, though, pots and pans have not caught on the way other kitchenwares have — except the well-known brand names such as Griswold and Wagner, for which the demand is almost as high as the price. Otherwise, the supply is abundant, and the prices are reasonable. If you're looking for an old pot or pan, check its overall condition, make sure its weight won't become a problem, and pay close attention to the handle attachment. It must be secure.

Note the condition of the inside of the pot, too. If it has a substantial mineral buildup, as is typical with aluminum ware, you may never get it completely clean. If you do, keeping those lime deposits under control could become more effort than owning the pot is worth. Also look for signs of scorching and burning. These could indicate that the pan has a tendency to get too hot, or that a hot spot exists.

The Benefits of Iron

You don't want lead leaching into your food from your cooking utensils, but a little leached iron from an old cast-iron skillet might be beneficial. According to experts at the American Dietetic Association, small amounts of iron from iron pots, pans, and skillets will absorb into your food. Unless you have a condition called *hemochromatosis*, in which excess iron in your system can cause serious problems, the small amount of iron you'll ingest from food cooked in an iron pot will not be harmful. If you're anemic, it could even be helpful.

Dad Despain's $5 garage sale find, this silver-plated serving pan, called a brazier, needed only a good polishing to restore it to its wonderful 1930s condition. A brazier, like a chafing dish, sat atop a heat source to keep its contents warm throughout a meal.

Mixing Bowls

Mixing bowls are downright abundant in antiques malls and flea markets. Because several different styles were so popular in the 1940s and 1960s, you can create complete sets, piece by piece, very inexpensively. Look for four-piece Pyrex bowl sets in varied sizes and colors, for example. These were among the most popular wedding gifts in the 1950s, and complete sets as well as orphan pieces can be found almost anywhere that vintage kitchenwares are sold. So can Fire King's white bowls with brightly painted fruits encircling them. They were big sellers in the 1960s, and many of these sets are still intact because of that success. Every good housewife had her own and now these bowls are being sold by original or second generation owners who are just tired of using them after all these years. Consequently, the abundant supply still existing means good prices.

My favorite Pyrex bowls, from Nana White's kitchen of course, have been in everyday use since 1947. They aren't especially old or of great monetary value, but the wonderful memories they hold go into everything mixed in them.

Earthenware bowls are also very popular, and while crockery predating the twentieth century is often too pricey for everyday use, earthenware made well into the twentieth century is a good, affordable alternative. If you can't tell the difference between antique and newer earthenware, let the asking price be your guide. Ten to thirty dollars is a reasonable amount to pay for a bowl you intend to use, and the bowl you get for that price probably won't be too old. Anything you spend over that amount is a matter of personal choice, but because many dealers don't know how to tell old earthenware from new, it's possible to buy something much newer than what you expected at a price more suited for something old.

These Fire King beauties found popularity in the 1960s and are now finding renewed popularity in collectibles circles. Their hand-painted flowers and fruits are lovely, and their value is sure to increase.

If a good old crockery bowl is just what you need, this 1930s example could be the one. It comes in two traditional colors, brown and blue.

IRONSTONE
A hard, white stoneware made by adding any of the various hard iron ores.

One warning about earthenware: *Never use for eating or drinking anything that's unglazed or that's glazing is chipped or substantially worn away.* This goes for coffee mugs, dinner plates, and any other piece of earthenware that may come into contact with food or beverages. Old earthenware as well as new imported reproductions often contain lead.

Dishes

Dishes are probably the most abundant kitchenwares out there. Their styles and prices range from casual and inexpensive to very fine and very expensive.

It's actually possible to find entire sets of antique or vintage china for sale at prices much lower than what you'd pay for an equivalent new set, but in general even the lower cost of vintage china as compared to new can be quite high. If you intend to purchase an entire set, identify a maker's mark on the back to ensure you aren't buying a reproduction, consult a book on vintage china, then count and check every piece for chips and cracks. And by all means insist that the dealer wrap every item separately for the ride home.

Maybe you'd like a set of better dishes but just can't afford fine china. Consider some of the nicer options for sale, such as the blue and white New England–pattern Currier and Ives dishes popular in the 1960s, or a vintage set of Ironstone, which resembles china but can be found at much less than half the price.

Another option if you want nice china but can't find the money for a complete set is to mix and match. Single settings can be found at reasonable prices. And who's to say you can't set a formal table using several different china patterns, anyway? The idea that each of your guests will have his or her own special place setting has aesthetic

appeal. Diners who return to your home often may even show a marked fondness for one particular pattern.

As for those everyday dishes, it's a buyer's market. Anything you can possibly imagine, and a few ugly pieces you've never dreamed of, is available. You'll find everything from old Melamine plates introduced in the late 1940s and popular through the 1960s to some of the hottest items on the collectibles market, including Fiestaware (dish sets that came in a variety of mix-and-match colors) and Jadite by Fire King (heavy jade-green glass dishes). Both of the latter are widely collected, pretty expensive, and maybe even inflated in price because of their current popularity. In the case of Fiestaware, new models are rolling off the assembly line right now. So if you decide to splurge on some of the more popular brands of vintage dish sets, find a book and do your homework first, or you may end up getting stung pretty heavily. (See page 205 for a list of references.)

Glasses

Like dishes, glasses come in all qualities and price ranges. You'll find fine sets of vintage or antique hand-blown glass stemware — and of everyday 1960s aluminum drinking tumblers. What you purchase is entirely

Fine china is nice but its high cost can be prohibitive. Consider another option — a great old Ironstone set such as this one looks beautiful and can be had for a fraction of the cost of china.

Finding complete sets of dishes or replacements isn't a problem in most antiques and collectibles shops. Kitchen collectibles sell well, so there's always lots from which to choose, including Jadite items like these. It's a buyer's market, so decide what you need and go to it!

a matter of taste and budget, because the supply of glasses is never ending.

Here's a buying secret that might interest the budget-conscious shopper: If you'd like the look of nice crystal glasses and dessert cups but can't afford the price, look for early-1960s reproductions listed as "peanut butter glass." Peanut butter was sold in some great-looking fake crystal years ago, and those pieces are now hitting the resale market in a big way. The price is quite low — a few dollars per glass — and unless your guests are crystal experts, you can fool them with what was once used as a gimmick to sell that plain or crunchy, stick-to-the-roof-of-your-mouth stuff.

Flatware

Again, the range is broad. You'll find sets of fine sterling (make sure you take your magnifying glass and look for the mark on the back indicating that it is indeed sterling), and you'll see everyday flatware. Pieces are often sold individually, and that's where you can find the real bargains if you want to take the time to hunt, and you don't mind a table full of orphans. But a lot of flatware is sold by the set. Count the pieces to make sure you're getting everything you expect; check the fork tines for straightness and equal length; and, while no one is looking, do a quick taste test. Some older flatware will have a metallic taste that's unpleasant, or simply one you're not used to. It would be unfortunate to purchase an entire set only to find you can't stand the taste of the eating utensil that will go into your mouth with every bite you take.

Odds and Ends

There are so many wonderful old objects that can be turned into something functional that it's nearly impossible to list them all. But here are a few of the really great ones:

- **Old flatirons** used for ironing make great doorstops or bookends.
- **Trivets** used to hold hot flatirons are attractive wall decorations and also a good place to put hot pots and pans.
- **Copper or aluminum food molds** look great hanging on the wall — and they can still be functional.
- **Canning jars,** especially the old green ones, are a particularly lovely way to store rice, beans, sugar, tea bags, or anything else that needs a tight container. Because they come in a variety of sizes, you can compile a complete set of them.
- **Wooden boxes** in which pasteurized processed cheese came are great little storage bins for spice tins, keys or pens and memo pads.
- **Old spice tins** are wonderful storage containers for new spices. Make sure you clean them out carefully before you fill them. If you buy one with a paper label or one that's made of cardboard, wipe the inside clean but take care to keep the outside dry. Never use the spices that come in old tins or other spice storage containers such as jars or bottles, as they could turn out to be something other than what is advertised on the label. Or, they might be inhabited by tiny critters, as many old spices are.

▲ Put one on the fire, heat it up, iron some clothes, then repeat. If you're a back to basics kind of person, a c. 1900 flatiron can still do a heck of a job on your clothes.

▲ It's just a wooden cheese box, one that predates the yellow cardboard variety we see in stores today. But it's a great place to hold kitchen odds and ends. If you buy one, make sure the writing or artwork is intact, because that's where the value is found.

▶ *Just because they're old doesn't mean these tins can't hold spices as they did forty years ago. Nowhere on the grocery store shelves can you find containers with the character of these classic tins.*

- **Ice tongs** can be used in place of traditional plastic paper towel holders. Hang one on your wall and hook the tongs through the paper towel roll. Just make sure the tongs separate easily before you make a purchase. Evaluate the handle for its hanging potential, too. Some varieties won't lie flat against the wall.
- **Old treadle sewing machine stands** make great microwave oven tables. Normally, the sewing machine itself has been removed; you're left with only the case. Sometimes that's even been taken off and replaced by some sort of tabletop mounted over the original iron legs. Whatever the form, the tables now made from old treadle sewing machines have many different uses, and because current market value for most intact treadle machines in their original stands is quite low, they're becoming popular items to purchase and modify. An especially good buy is one with all its original drawers.
- **An old shutter,** mounted flat to the wall with hooks screwed into the bottom edge, can be a wonderful place to hang your pots and pans.

Even if it doesn't serve its primary purpose anymore, an old-fashioned sewing machine can have several modern-day uses. This early twentieth-century model is perfectly happy holding an early twenty-first century microwave.

Kitchen and Dining Room Furniture

Think about the chair on which you'd like to sit while you eat prime rib from the vintage fine china you just purchased, or sup wine from that peanut butter glass. Then give some thought to the table that will hold all the food that's waiting to be served in your attractive set of hand-painted Fire King bowls. Or maybe you need a hutch or old-fashioned sideboard (piece of dining room furniture for holding articles of table service) in which to store your newfound dishes.

Dining room and kitchen furniture are both plentiful in most antiques and collectibles outlets, and the prices are usually right. If you aren't a stickler about traditional form, the prices can get even better. For example, if you like the eclectic mismatched look of a table and chairs that are not part of the same set, you can buy orphaned pieces for a fraction of what you'd pay for a complete set. People customarily want their table and chairs matched, so mismatched pieces have little collectible value — a fact usually reflected in a low price. And these days, the mix-and-match look is very trendy in kitchen and even formal dining room furniture. One table with six or eight different and unique chairs: What better way to make dinner guests feel special and individual?

Next, make sure that every chair you purchase has its seat set at exactly the same height from the floor. A table full of guests seated at all different levels can be awkward and embarrassing. Think about it for a moment. Wouldn't you be offended if you ended up sitting several inches lower than the person next to you?

Moving away from formal dining furniture, consider some of the kitchen options. Chrome tables that reached their peak of popularity in the 1950s are still available at good prices. In fact, many that have been in continual use for the past fifty years are — like so many other vintage kitchenware pieces of that time — just beginning to enter the marketplace. If you come across one and think you might buy it, check the chrome legs and trim carefully for signs of repainting, and for dents and dings. Also check the stability, making sure the table isn't wobbly or a leg uneven. Run your hand over the tabletop to feel for a smooth, undamaged surface. Take a look at the

Consider How Things Fit

Don't just buy at random if you decide to create your own personal dining room or kitchen set. Measure first the height of the table, and then the height of the chair in relationship to it, to make sure one fits comfortably with the other. Nothing is more inconvenient than sitting at a table in a chair that's too low or high.

chairs; a vintage chrome table may not have all of its chairs, and you might have to mix and match. The chairs that did come with the set — in case you do find them — consisted of a vinyl seat and back mounted to a chrome frame.

Another popular kitchen option is an enamel-topped table with fold-out wings. These tables were highly popular in the 1940s and are in great demand for those wishing to create a retro kitchen. Originally, most of the tabletops were white; the trim was painted red or blue. Other bright colors were used, too, so inspect these tables carefully to make sure the paint is original. Be very judicious, though. Chipped enamel can be repaired by kits found in most hardware stores, and many of these older tables have been repaired. Repaired enamel will greatly reduce the resale value of the table, if you should decide to sell it someday, so be aware of what you're buying before you buy it. Also, pay attention to nicks that haven't been repaired. They should lower the cost of the table considerably, possibly by

Seek, and You Shall Find

When you're hunting for a table, don't overlook anything. The table on which several knickknacks or kitchen items are arranged for sale may itself be for sale. Most people forget to look at the object on which other objects are displayed, and that's a mistake because it's often where the real bargains can be found.

Sometimes dealers overlook their own means of display, and great pieces of furniture can sit for several years with an old, outdated price tag, simply because everyone has overlooked it as an item for sale. For example, one avid shopper found a two-hundred-year-old, solid-cherry, drop-leaf table for $100 because he remembered to look at the display table as well as the items for sale on it. The price tag was almost completely faded with age, and the dealer even admitted he'd forgotten the piece was for sale. The market value for such a table at the time was about four to five times that price, and the shopper walked away very happy with his deal.

as much as half. A table in perfect condition can still be found for around $100 in many areas of the United States, so a slightly damaged piece can be a real bargain, especially if you can live with a chip or you know how to fix it.

After you've taken care of your table and chairs, think about buying a hutch or sideboard for storage. These pieces look nice in a formal setting and also serve a practical purpose. They can fit into other spaces, too — a living room, wide hallway, den, or bedroom — if your dining room is too small. Again, you'll pay a higher price for matched items but substantially less for orphaned pieces. The best buys start in furniture made about thirty years after the turn of the twentieth century, and some of the most reasonably priced hutches date from the 1950s and 1960s. Older antique dining room furniture, including orphaned pieces, is currently at an all-time high market value; on top of that, hutches and sideboards are being reproduced to look like older ones. So when you decide to invest in an antique piece, check for indications of wear and age before you sign the check.

LIVING AREAS

Dens, family rooms, living rooms, and any other places where your family congregates should overflow with comfort, but *comfort* is a relative term. For some it's a spacious, open area with few furnishings. For others it's cozy and cluttered. However you choose your comfort, the place in which you spend most of your waking hours should suit your needs — without compromise. For example, Victorian parlor and living room furniture is

Some of the greatest buys in dining room furniture come from the 1950s, such as this hutch. Found in an antiques mall with a price tag of $300, it's in perfect condition, without a scratch or blemish.

beautiful, if you like that style, and there's no doubt it looks lovely in many settings, but most of it was not made for comfort. It was rigid enough for formal use — which is fine if that's your intended use for it, too. But if it's not, think again. An old Victorian chair is rarely something in which you'd curl up and get comfortable, and if you buy one thinking you can endure its lack of comfort for the sake of its beauty, be sure your greatest need is looks and not comfort. Know, without a doubt, that you can live with the compromise you're about to make, because after a long, hard day at work when all you want to do is go home and get comfortable, there won't be any comfort or cozy time in that Victorian chair.

Furniture

Shopping for comfort pieces — couches, overstuffed chairs — isn't always easy in antiques and collectibles

Mistaken Mahogany?

Buyer beware! Wonderful, complete dining room sets can be found in many of the finer antiques malls, and are also sold at the better shows. Currently, deep, rich mahogany products are among the most popular and sell for top dollar. That expensive-looking furniture, however, could be brand new, imported from Indonesia just last week.

Many dealers are resorting to selling these brand-new imports and attaching the price tag that should be affixed to fine older antiques — a much higher price than a new import commands. So if you're considering a mahogany piece, be careful. Make sure it's vintage, and ask the dealer for an affidavit stating that it is — and that in the event it's proven otherwise, your money will be refunded in full. Too many unsuspecting buyers are being duped by this furniture because dealers are mingling it with antiques and collectibles. It's fine furniture and looks good in many homes, but you have the right to know what you're buying. Don't pay a premium-antique price for something that's not.

venues. Unless these pieces are considered antique or high-quality vintage, they usually go to a used-furniture dealer. Some, however, end up in places you might shop; if you can find them, you'll probably also find a pretty good bargain. If it's the traditional fabric-covered stuffed sofa and chairs you're after, though, exercise some caution before you hand over the money, no matter how good the deal. Many people have made what they think is a great buy only to find more than they bargained for when they get home. This furniture can:

- **Be insect infested.** Smell for any signs of insecticide. Pull out cushions and look for bug droppings, and don't hesitate to use your magnifying glass. In summer, when fleas are in season, sit down on the furniture for a while to see if any of those little critters decide to visit you. It won't take them long to come out to greet you if they're there.
- **Have remnants of pet life.** Look for fabric stains. Pull up the cushions and take a whiff. Inspect legs and the underneath sides for urine stains. If the piece is heavily cloaked in a coverup scent, be wary. You could be buying something that will eventually overpower the masking scent to reek of old cat urine.
- **Have remnants of human life.** Check for stains under the seat cushions. Again, take a whiff. Do you detect cigarettes or body odor? Does the piece smell heavily of one of those coverup aerosols?
- **Have untoward contours.** Also check the condition of the fabric or leather and the contours of the seat cushions and back. You may not care to sit in the exact body indentations of the previous owner, but if the piece has been well used, any indentations might be permanent.

Clean Your Furniture

Even if the furniture you just bought seems spotless, consider having it cleaned professionally before you start to live with or on it. If there are some problems you did not detect, a good cleaning will probably fix them. And in all honesty, since you really don't know what transpired on that sofa before you bought it, do you really want to cozy up on it until you know it's clean?

Wooden furniture doesn't come with the hygiene warnings, fortunately, and often the only thing you need to do to is wipe it with a light coat of furniture oil. Most leading commercial brands will do the trick, and often you can find furniture oil specifically for antiques and vintage pieces offered for sale at antiques malls and flea markets.

Granted, there are some strong warnings attached to buying vintage cloth-covered furniture, but that's not to say you can't find a good buy in great shape, because you can. And you'll often come across pieces that have been re-covered for resale. Just make sure you do your best Sherlock Holmes impression and check out every inch before you buy anything.

If you're not sure you want to buy vintage or previously used comfort furniture, consider sticking with new pieces or those you already own, then adding antiques and collectibles around them. Coffee tables, accent tables, desks, wooden rocking chairs or benches, and display units such as china cabinets or hutches look great in almost any decor. And if you want to add a little practicality to your living area, consider replacing some of those end tables or coffee tables with old steamer trunks. The kind with flat lids are usually on the lower end of the price scale, and they offer you both inside storage and a flat surface on which to display more of your treasures.

Old trunks, such as this wooden turn-of-the-century beauty from the 1900s, can serve a multitude of purposes today: Use it for storage, as a coffee table, or as a display surface.

Another popular substitute for the common living room table is the kind of old spool cabinet once used for holding thread. This is the right height for an accessory table and usually comes with three to five drawers. Currently, market values for the very best examples — those with original finish and that feature an intact thread advertisement on the cabinet — are quite high and moving upward. However, lesser-quality cabinets with their all-important advertisement missing, or with wood that has been repainted or refinished in some manner, can still be found at reasonable prices. If you decide to purchase an example that seems in perfect condition, though, be aware that some dealers are duplicating missing or damaged advertising. A great old spool cabinet in perfect original condition can be a good investment and wonderful addition to your home, but make sure you're getting what you think you are.

Old washstands are a good addition to living space, too, and prices, in many cases, are still quite reasonable.

Smaller examples, such as those made for children, can serve in the place of a little accessory table, plus they have drawers and a storage space underneath. Larger examples can stand alone as anything you want them to be — a place to display knickknacks, a storage unit, a piece of furniture to fill up a wall. And if it's drawers you need, consider a desk. These come in all varieties, from primitive to student, and they can function as anything from a work desk to a table or storage unit. Small ones will fit into a small space and be unobtrusive in a room,

Before indoor plumbing, having a weekly bath was quite a chore and required toting water in from the pump, heating it, filling the tub, and emptying the tub. Daily grooming was done from the washstand. This one, c. 1875, is without its original mirror. Today, it houses my cookbook collection.

and large ones can become a centerpiece. When you purchase a desk:

- ◆ Make sure that the drawers slide in and out easily, and that the space in which the unit will sit has adequate room for each drawer's full extension.
- ◆ See that it sits level on the floor. Even a tiny lean one way or the other can cause books you intend to display on your desk to slide.
- ◆ Make sure the chair you'll use with it is neither too high nor too low.

Bookshelves and knickknack shelves also fit nicely into living areas, and they can be used for other collectibles as well as books. Entire bookshelf units can be purchased, but make sure of the overall height before you do. Check the plane of the shelf, too. Old wood warps, so be sure the shelf is level before you buy it, especially if you intend to use it for knickknacks. Single shelf units,

This c. 1945 student desk is small, simple, and looks great in an out-of-the-way corner. The drawers and all that wonderful storage are the best part. This particular desk was offered for sale in an antiques mall for $95.

old boards, and wooden bed rails also make great displays. If you're into the casual look, buy several old wooden shipping crates and stack them on their sides around and on top of each other. You might consider mounting them to a wall with a nail or screw for stability's sake, since they probably won't sit flush with each other.

Anything with a flat surface and narrow width can be converted into a shelf of some sort. The top of an old wooden ironing board would look great in a laundry room or kitchen; an old shutter could dress up a family room or enclosed porch. Use your imagination. If it's flat, not too deep, and can be attached to the wall or stacked freestanding, it certainly has the potential to be a display or storage shelf.

Hallways and Stairways

These narrow places make interesting decorating challenges. They do have decorating potential, but they're limited in space, so whatever you choose for either area must reflect that lack of space. If it doesn't, you'll be tripping over your own feet and bumping into walls trying to pass through that narrow walkway.

Consider your stairs first. Certainly whatever you choose for decorating them should have a narrow profile so the walking space isn't compromised. Many people like baskets or artificial flower arrangements to adorn their steps, but these can make navigation difficult, especially for those who have a walking impairment to begin with. Instead, place baskets on the floor at the bottom of the stairs or on a landing, and concentrate on the walls along the steps. A sconce looks good opposite the railing. So might a small collection of wall pockets

Nana White's 1930s wall pockets have held everything from fresh flowers to potted ivy. She also hid candy and other small gifts in them on special occasions.

Booze bottles like these can quickly become a specialty collection because they are available in so many wonderful colors, sizes, and shapes. Because they were quite popular sixty to eighty years ago, you can find them almost everywhere.

(wall-hanging vases designed to sit flat against the wall.) Another nice, flat decorating option is a group of the old violin and banjo bottles that were so popular back in the 1920s. Some came with whiskey and others were made specifically for decoration, but good examples of these bottles are found in every color of the rainbow, their current prices are reasonable, and they look great just about anywhere.

Think about putting a small table on the landing for a few family photos, if you haven't already hung them on the wall leading up the stairs. An old treadle sewing machine converted into a table will work, too, if there's enough room. So will an old wooden stool, or even a couple of stacked wooden storage boxes or crates. After all, a table doesn't really have to be a table. It can be anything on which something else can sit.

Hallways offer a little more decorating leeway than stairs, but the walking area still must not be impeded, so whatever you choose should also have a minimal profile. Small tables always look nice. So does an array of floor items such as crocks, graniteware, or anything else that strikes your fancy. Mirrors, pictures, and lighting can also adorn your walls. A great lamp choice that's still found in many venues and looks wonderful anywhere you put it is a bracket-and-reflector oil lamp. It has aesthetic uses, but it will also light the way when the power goes out. Antique hall lamps are also great items to place in hallways, especially those with high ceilings. These old oil lamps feature a pulley mechanism that drops down from the ceiling when you wish to light the lamp, then raises back up and out of the way. Both beautiful and functional, good hall lights are scarce collectibles that are expensive and still going up in price. Still, a complete light that hasn't been converted to electricity may well be worth the few hundred dollars you spend on it.

If you like to line your halls with old family photos, think about moving those photos into old frames. Just make sure you have an idea what frame sizes you'll need before you buy. Don't worry if you find chipping, distress marks, and holes left from gnawing insects on the frames you purchase; these merely add character. Also, since the value of an old frame isn't too great to begin with, there's no reason to seek out something in perfect condition unless you simply prefer perfect over a well-used look.

Keep a watchful eye wherever you go! This favorite oil lamp was hanging high in the rafters of an antiques mall when I discovered it.

Making Use of Mantels

Old fireplace mantels are often offered for sale in antiques and collectibles venues, and if you're considering building a home with a fireplace, make sure you shop several places selling architectural antiques before you make up your mind. But what if you're already living in a home without a fireplace, and you've found a mantel you love? Create a space for it. A small mantel can be put in a hallway to use as a shelf. Mounted on the wall, a fireplace mantel can be an attractive conversation piece as well as a great place for a few knick-knacks to sit. It might look nice in a bedroom, too, or any other place where you'd like to create a cozy atmosphere.

BEDROOMS

Nowhere is your comfort more important than in your bedroom, but if your bedroom is like that of most people, its space is limited. The room dimensions are small, storage availability inadequate, and unused wall and floor area at a premium. But you still need the basics — the bed, the dresser, the chest of drawers, and an armoire if you can squeeze it in. A blanket chest is always nice, too, and maybe you'd like a slipper chair or tiny rocking chair. Take everything you want in your bedroom into consideration before you start to buy, and list the pieces according to priority. When you do, keep these things in mind:

- ◆ Room dimensions
- ◆ The width of the door, halls, and entryways leading to the bedroom
- ◆ The function and necessity of the pieces you want

Now think about the furniture piece by piece.

Your Bed

Because so many bedrooms just aren't as large as they need to be, establish your bed priorities before you shop. Think about:

- ◆ **Users.** Who will use the bed?
- ◆ **Size.** What size do you need and how much space is available for it?
- ◆ **Other furniture pieces.** Will your bed be part of a matched set or an orphan?
- ◆ **Sturdiness.** You don't want a rickety bed, so make sure the frame is sturdy. If the bed isn't assembled, ask whether the dealer, mall manager, or you can assemble it. Make sure the joints fit together well, too.

- **Height.** Older beds were higher than most constructed today. In fact, some were so high that you needed a two-step stool to climb into them. Be confident that you won't mind the climb if you fall in love with a bed that requires a step stool.
- **Slats.** Many older beds don't come with slats; you'll have to make your own. Be sure the bed rails will be adequate to support your added slats.
- **Noise.** Some frames squeak. Manipulate the frame back and forth to see if the sounds it makes will bother you or the person sleeping in the next room.

When you browse antiques and collectibles outlets, you'll commonly find beds collapsed and stashed over to the side, against a wall or partway behind other things. They take up so much room that a dealer simply can't afford to display them any other way. So if you see what appears to be a stray dresser or chest of drawers, look around. The matching bed could be hiding. And if you're looking for an orphaned bed, it's probably collapsed and half hidden, too.

After you've made your bed selection, apply the same standards of evaluation and quality you desire to every other piece of furniture that will go into your bedroom.

Your Dresser and Chest of Drawers

Now that you've settled on a bed, think about a dresser or chest of drawers. Typically, a dresser is lower than a chest, and features a long attached mirror in which to see yourself when you dress. It's not uncommon to find a dresser without a mirror, but that's probably not the way it was made. Often, when bedroom furniture was

---

Mattresses Matter

Never buy a used mattress, even if it's labeled antique. In most states, selling a used mattress is illegal. Invest your collectibles money in a good bed frame, then buy a brand-new mattress to fit into it.

Great Finds for Your Bedroom

The Jenny Lind bed, marked by decoratively turned spindles in the headboard and footboard, has been popular and reproduced for well over a century. This style, in fact — named for a popular Swedish singer who toured the United States with showman P. T. Barnum in the 1850s — has finally taken its place in the classic category. New examples are produced today and vary little from those produced a hundred or more years ago. And the best thing about a Jenny Lind bed is that it can be paired with almost any style of dresser or armoire and still looks great.

The waterfall style of furniture, popular in the 1930s, is characterized by well-rounded edges resembling the flow of a waterfall, and usually made with an elaborate wood-grained veneer. Inlays of contrasting veneer were a popular decoration, as were attractive brass drawer handles and pulls.

Waterfall furniture saw its rise and fall from popularity in just a few years, and examples purchased new sixty or seventy years ago are just now beginning to find their way into the resale circles. Vintage waterfall furniture has not caught on as a popular collectible yet, so prices are still reasonable. You may be able to find an entire five-piece suite for just a few hundred dollars. This style's day will come, however, and the prices will go up. And it won't be long until it is a genuine antique.

replaced, the mirror was removed and hung elsewhere. Some were made to be removed, others merely cut off. So if you find the perfect dresser, but it lacks a mirror, check the back closely for any signs that a mirror was once attached. If the evidence is there — usually in the form of wooden support pieces that have been cut off at the height of the dresser top — don't pay book value for the piece. Point out the missing mirror to the dealer and ask for a discount, because furniture altered in such a manner retains only a fraction of its intact value. There's nothing wrong with buying an altered piece, though, especially if you can get it at a reduced price. And if you do go home with a mirrorless dresser, you can always hang a separate old mirror on the wall in the place the attached one should be.

If you need a vanity table for makeup and other dressing chores, consider using an old wooden desk or treadle sewing machine case with drawers, then hanging a mirror on the wall above it. The drawer space will be more than double what you'll find in an actual vanity; there may well be more legroom under it, too. You can also use an old wooden table with a drawer or two.

A chest of drawers is a good bet for a bedroom, and there are as many styles as there are tastes in furniture. Traditional highboy examples are always available and offer huge storage potential. They are quite tall, however — often too tall for a modern home with an average ceiling height. They can also be taller than you can reach, an inconvenient situation. If you don't like the idea of dragging a step stool every time you want something from the top drawer, consider something lower and more suited to your height.

Your primary considerations when buying a chest of drawers should be size, ease of use — some have huge

This c. 1800 solid cherry dresser was weighted down with collectibles, but its dusty, faded price tag caught my eye. It's a beautiful, functional addition to my guest room.

drawers that are difficult to pull — and how it looks with your other furniture. One caution, though: Because old chests of drawers are among the most practical pieces of antique or vintage furniture for sale, prices can be a bit high. Pieces predating the twentieth century often carry a price tag that reflects their age. Some of the better buys come in dressers made twenty to thirty years after the turn of the twentieth century.

Other Storage Pieces

Armoires were made for storage, pure and simple. They held clothes, blankets, and anything else that needed to be stashed away. Older homes, even some built well into the twentieth century, often lacked ample closet space. Many were not constructed with closets at all, because armoires were the closets.

Today armoire lovers consider these huge pieces of furniture as attractive ways to store the overflow from their closets. Armoires are also a nice way to display collectibles. Here are some more bedroom storage ideas:

- ◆ Steamer trunks
- ◆ Sea chests (marked by domed lids)

Immigrants' chests like this one were brought to our shores from the Old World, holding the cherished belongings of an individual or an entire family. This chest began its life with the Zugenbein family in Germany and found its way to the Despain household in Indiana 300 years later.

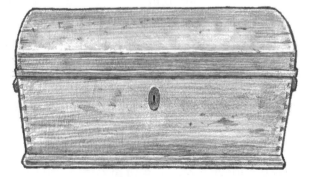

Armoire or Entertainment Center?

Many armoires are converted into entertainment centers. Unfortunately, while they certainly lend themselves to that function with some changes to the basic structure, cutting holes in the back to accommodate electronic equipment will reduce their antique value. If you're seeking an entertainment center and stumble across a converted armoire, by all means buy it, but don't cut up one that's intact unless you're prepared to take a financial loss of as much as 75 percent that will come with the alteration.

- Cedar-lined chests and blanket chests
- Orphaned drawers (attach some wheels and slide under the bed for shoe storage)
- Old wooden boxes or crates with lids
- Vintage hard-sided luggage

Bedroom Chairs

What type of chair you put in your bedroom will depend on how much space you have left over. Any type of chair will do so long as you have a use for it. Traditional bedroom-type chairs include:

- **Vanity chairs** allow you to sit in front of the vanity or dresser. Make sure yours is the right height for the furniture it will complement.
- **Slipper chairs,** popular in the 1930s, are low to the ground, with a wide seat and low back. Their intended use was for sitting while putting on shoes and slippers.

Armoires are free-standing closets that can hold virtually anything. This early nineteenth-century armoire makes an exceedingly practical linen closet.

Nana White spent nearly 95 years rocking in one or the other of these chairs. The Boston rocker (left) sat in the living room and the bedroom rocker (right) was always next to her bed. If you listen closely, you can still hear her rocking gently.

♦ **Bedroom rockers** are much smaller than regular rocking chairs and were popular prior to the turn of the twentieth century. They were used by women who wanted to sit alongside the bed to sew or mend clothing, or to watch over a sick child or husband.

You don't have to be bound by tradition, though, and any chair that suits your fancy will work in your bedroom. Just make sure it's comfortable if you want to sit in it for more than a few minutes at a time. And if you think the chair will become a catchall for clothes, belts, and whatever else you toss in its direction, consider buying something that isn't too expensive, or that won't scratch. All those gizmos and gadgets that might end up on the chair could take a toll, and you really don't want a belt buckle to scratch your prized nineteenth-century chair, or an ink pen to leak on it, do you?

BATHROOMS

Yes, even the bathroom can get an antiques once-over. Granted, its space is limited, and so is its decorating potential, but apart from your basic tub, toilet, and sink, there are a few nice things you can do to make your bathroom comfortable. First, consider a vintage sink. Old porcelain pedestal models can be found at many antiques malls and shows, and a store specializing in one of the fastest-growing antiques and collectibles specialties — architectural antiques — is sure to have just the old sink you want. You might even find that old claw-foot bathtub, too, although in good shape that's a bathroom piece that comes with a hefty price tag. Still, if you want to splurge, vintage bathroom mainstays are available and popular.

Apart from the tub and sink, a few other collectibles ideas can turn an ordinary bathroom into a comfortable one. Remember the old ice tong used for paper towels? It can be used with toilet paper, too. And don't forget a few old medicine bottles, vintage soaps, shaving items, old perfume bottles, and other items typically found in the medicine cabinet. They make wonderful displays. One cautionary note, however: Avoid decorative paper products in your bathroom. Over time, steam from the shower can ruin them. If you find an old box of Ivory soap that you must display no matter what, either keep it as far away from a moisture source as possible or cover it in plastic wrap, and don't allow any of the tape's adhesive to touch the original packaging.

Check out a vintage-linens booth, too. Maybe you'll be lucky enough to stumble across some old fingertip towels that were typically embroidered as an add-on then presented as wedding or bridal shower gifts. They're still available and, because they haven't found their market yet, the prices are reasonable. Handmade crocheted doilies also look nice in the bathroom, as well as any other room in the house.

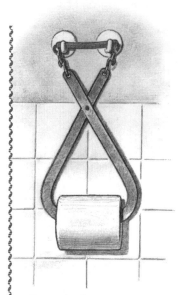

Does the iceman cometh? No more, but his tongs make an interesting and functional addition to my bathroom.

ARCHITECTURAL ANTIQUES AND COLLECTIBLES

As mentioned earlier in this chapter, architectural antiques are one of the fastest-growing areas in home collectibles. And the category is so vast it covers everything from doors to doorknobs, floor molding to stained-glass windows. Virtually anything that once found a place in an

Outdoor Accents

Architectural antiques are among the most popular pieces for outdoor decoration, and come in the form of:

- Urns
- Cement statuary, including benches and other lawn ornaments
- Copper downspouts
- Flower boxes

This turn-of-the-century solid brass keyhole plate cost only $1, and even though it no longer hangs on a door, it adds texture and life to a wall decorated with other similar knickknacks.

old home and has been salvaged is an architectural antique or collectible. Most people buy them to fit into their existing homes, but others will actually design a home to fit an architectural piece they have already purchased.

For the everyday budget, many architectural pieces are out of reach. There are, however, many nice things that are still priced reasonably enough to make a wonderful addition to your home. Take a look at this list for a few ideas:

- Brass hinges
- Brass or glass doorknobs
- Brass keyhole plates
- Stained- or beveled-glass windows
- Doors
- Fireplace mantels
- Columns
- Bathroom and kitchen fixtures
- Tile

Other outdoor collectibles often available where architectural pieces are sold include wrought-iron furniture and old wooden and metal lawn furniture. While these are not technically architectural pieces, they're seeing an increase in popularity — and in price.

Can you picture yourself entertaining guests in your garden on a warm spring afternoon? Now imagine them resting comfortably seated on classic wrought-iron furniture, sipping lemonade. Ah!

What about Lightning Rods?

Old lightning rods with ornamental glass balls are some of the most consistently popular architectural collectibles. Designed to attract lightning and send it straight into the ground through a wire lead, these rods sat prominently on the top of most old farmhouses and barns through the 1930s, with some structures adorned by several at a time.

The glass balls accompanying the rod — collectibles themselves these days — were sold from door to door by salesmen, and came in a choice of colors and styles, with the guarantee that if lightning were ever to strike the rod, the ball would break, thus alerting the homeowner of the near miss. Often, as it turned out, the salesman would return weeks later only to point out one or more broken glass balls. Then he'd sell the home-owner another set to replace the broken ones. Rumor has it that the most enterprising and successful lightning rod salesmen were gun-toting sure shots who would shoot the glass balls themselves to guarantee future sales.

Old lightning rods complete with weather vanes and glass balls are great architectural collectibles to put back up on the roof, but the cost of the balls can become prohibitive for use out-doors. The rods themselves are inexpensive, so if you like the idea of an old-time lightning rod sitting atop your house, give some thought to an original rod with a repro-duction ball (just in case that old salesman happens by and decides to take aim once again). These repros are available from most dealers specializing in old glass, par-ticularly old bottles.

This early twentieth-century lightning rod and ball sits atop my desk amid my papers. I purchased it with my first writing paycheck, and I've not been struck by lightning yet!

Odds and Ends

There are so many things that can make your home more comfortable, it's impossible to list every single one. An old woodstove might look great in your kitchen as a place to stash pots and pans or hold your microwave; if it's intact and functional, it can also be used in case of an emergency. A narrow wooden church pew might be just the thing to place in your entry hall or den, and maybe a telephone bench is just what you need in the family room. Perhaps a vintage high chair complete with your dad's old 1923 baby food dish will be useful for your baby, and think about hanging your grandma's old quilt on the wall to cover up a huge empty space.

Whatever you chose can be just what you want it to be, no matter if it's functional or aesthetic, traditional or odd. As long as you like it, that's all that counts.

Just add a stovepipe and ceiling vent, and this old beauty is ready to cook. It can serve as a fireplace, too, or take the place of a brand-new woodstove that may cost nearly twice the price.

Gallery of Decorating Ideas

When British poet Samuel Taylor Coleridge (1772–1834) said, "A picture is an intermediate something between a thought and a thing," he provided the perfect segue to this gallery of photographs, because they probably will fall somewhere between your thoughts about decorating and how you will actually decorate. Simply put, these photographs are meant to inspire. There are no rules or limits to what you can achieve when you apply your imagination. An old bottle turned lamp, flat irons used for book ends — anything is possible. So study these pages, think creatively, and decorate!

▲ The mark of a truly creative kitchen is functional versatility. Unused space can become display space. Odd-sized vintage utensils are always at-the-ready and add visual interest when placed on a contemporary shelf like this one, behind the stovetop. The old green fruit bowl looks perfectly content, too, even though it's a hundred years older than the counter-top on which it sits. Be brave! Be inventive! Your antiques and collectibles can work well anywhere.

▶ Vintage kitchen tools like these have endured and demonstrate their dependability every day. If you love vintage kitchenware and utensils like I do, don't be afraid to use them. An antique ice cream scoop, bread knife, and dry measure might be just what you need to make your modern kitchen complete.

▲ Whether used for storage or display, canning jars have a long tradition of service and can add beauty and a touch of whimsy anywhere in your home.

▶ Yes, these old wooden utensils still have what it takes to earn their keep in the kitchen. And, clearly, they're simply too beautiful to hide in a drawer.

▼ Old tins are growing in popularity because they have intricate designs, character, and history that new ones lack. Small or large groupings of tins provide a visual feast for the eyes.

◀ If preparing an item for display, consider a background color that brings out the best in the piece. The rose color of this built-in shelving complements the Japanese porcelain beautifully. A blue background probably would have made the display too dark; if set against a white background, many of the porcelain's delicate patterns would have disappeared. Experiment with background colors to see what works best for your particular piece.

▶ An eclectic display can catch the eye and add visual interest to a functional work space. The tea cups, vases, plates, and pitchers showcased above this rolltop desk invite closer inspection and offer the would-be writer or the reluctant bill preparer many lovely objects for contemplation.

▶ The great thing about having everyday antiques in your home is that each piece has a place, even a formal tea service such as this. The bygone rules of formal elegance no longer apply. Create your own style of elegance by mixing a few upper-end antiques with your not-so-upper-end collectibles. You'll be amazed by the beautiful results.

◀ Sterling silver spoons are sometimes hidden in a pile of silver-plated ones at an antiques show or flea market, just waiting for an astute eye to notice the difference. Hanging in a spoon rack, they'll dress up any wall, but don't forget to use these unique beauties when company comes a' calling.

▶ The styles for mantel clocks are almost as varied as the settings in which they are placed. Nestled in the corner of a country-style buffet or sitting prominently on a fire-place mantel, antique and vintage clocks are decorative and practical. Honor the clock maker's art by including at least one of these lovely pieces in your home.

▼ The best clock is one that works well, that looks beautiful, and that you love despite its follies and foibles. It doesn't have to be made by one of the great clock makers of the world, either. A primitive like this one can be as graceful and valuable to you as a clock with a notable pedigree.

▲ Nothing quite compares to the calm persistence of a clock ticking and its solemn tolling of the hours.

▶ Shelves are always at the ready to serve, displaying both practical and whimsical objects with aplomb. Here a phone-and-letter center shares space with pitchers, a plant, a serving tray, and lovely canisters.

▼ A cubbyhole is a small, enclosed place, and there's nothing more intriguing than cubbyholes stashed full of tiny antiques and collectibles. If you don't have any cubbyholes and need some desperately, consider hanging an old wooden printer's tray from the wall.

◄ The English poet George Herbert said, "Love the sea, but keep on the land." If you're a full-time land lover but a sailor at heart, there's an ocean full of nautical collectibles awaiting your display, from brass sextants and lanterns to life preservers and blown glass floats.

▶ The appeal is rustic, and it's not just for hunters anymore. Today, old wooden decoys sit on shelves, in floor groupings next to the fireplace, and anywhere else the call of the wild has a place in your home. As an added bonus, these pets are quiet, clean, and need nothing more than a good dusting every now and then.

172

▲ It may be disconcerting to see some of your favorite childhood toys for sale at several hundred times the original asking price in an antiques shop, but that's precisely what's happening, especially to old toys in original packaging that are in great shape. So keep your toys! Display them, and enjoy them as much as you did when you were young.

▶ If your toys are too fragile for little hands to touch, arrange them in a display case for all to see. And inspire a child's sense of wonder by sharing stories about these family treasures.

◀ Make your private space as personal and comfortable as you wish. Incorporate the things that make you feel good and that are pleasing to your eye. Whether you're decorating a reading nook or an office, make it a part of yourself and you'll be happy to go there again and again.

▶ Whether used in a hall as a decoration, just inside your front door as a place to drop your coat, or in a breakfast nook to replace traditional chairs, a wooden church pew is highly functional and can go just about anywhere. Sizes and styles vary, too.

▲ Even an old closet can become one of your favorite places. Remove the door, add a shelf to serve as a desk, then pull up an old chair, hang a few of your favorite things on the wall, add some lighting, and you'll have a cozy work space for writing, studying, sewing — whatever your heart desires.

▶ It might surprise you to find out that old Singers like this one still work. The stitches aren't as fancy as the ones from newer machines and the speed may be a bit slower, but there's certainly much to be said for creating something new from something old.

▲ Coverlets, such as this one from the nineteenth century, came in a variety of colors, blue and white being among the most popular. White wool was dyed with indigo in a kettle over an open fire, spun into yarn, then woven on a loom.

▶ This brand-new log cabin pattern quilt is a perfect match, in both color and style, for the nineteenth century bed — a lovely example of blending venerable with contemporary.

176

► What was once a washstand is now an incidental table used to hold just about anything. Arrange a few knickknacks or books on it, use it as a dressing table, or reintroduce it to its original purpose and stock it with the bath items it held one hundred years ago.

▼ Since the seventeenth century, blue and white has consistently been one of the most popular color combinations used in home decorating items and dishes. Mix and match your pieces for a truly stunning display.

177

◄ Paintings evoke so many different feelings that they don't have to be by Renoir or Matisse to become a cherished part of your home. Group them together in a panoramic view, or hang them separately. However you choose to display them, keep them out of direct light or they'll fade. And if you are so inclined, find a conservator to clean them if the years have dulled or darkened them.

► Keep your favorite photographs in your favorite places. Whether displayed on an old chest in an informal room like this or placed on the piano, wash stand, or fireplace mantel, photographs add life and love to any room. Vintage photos in period frames make lovely additions to almost any room, too.

▲ Walls aren't just for paintings and photos anymore. They're perfect showcases for anything that looks good on them — from old game boards to cowbells to rug beaters. But what about organ pipes? It's true that virtually anything will look beautiful in the right setting. These wooden organ pipes are delightful, unexpected conversation pieces.

▲ Shelves, again — the truest test of a fertile imagination. Nothing looks as warm and inviting as a shelf full of treasured memories, so don't limit yourself to books, even though books do look great. Bring out some of the family heirlooms, and buy a few new heirlooms for future generations. Show off the things you love the most.

▲ It doesn't require much to re-create an authentic rustic look. And the beauty of it is, nothing has to be in pristine shape. Rusty is good. Dented is fine. Well-used is wonderful. A cozy, rustic setting is one where everything in it has seen use of many years.

◄ Nothing is more captivating than the patina of old pewter and copper. But don't polish it away. That aged look bears witness to years of use, and that's exactly what you want. When cleaning such objects, wipe off the dust with a dry cloth, but not too vigorously.

Finishing Touches

by now you've found all the major pieces you really need to make your home a comfortable place in which to live — a bedroom suite, kitchen table, china closet, rocking chair. They're arranged in their rightful places and quickly becoming a treasured part of your home, maybe even your life. All things considered, perhaps now is a good time to look for the accent pieces and accessories — those unique touches that add beauty and warmth to the wonderful purchases you've already made. It's your chance to move away from the practical items on which you've spent so much time concentrating and try something a more little whimsical.

Maybe you can find a vintage Jell-O ad, frame it, and hang it on the kitchen wall. Or perhaps you'll buy a nice dresser bottle for the washstand. And while you're out there hunting for accessories, think also about your friends and what they might like from the antiques mall. As you're now aware, antiques and collectibles are fast becoming popular gifts items for almost every occasion, and no doubt you have a friend or two with enthusiasm for vintage pieces that matches your own.

LIGHTING

It's as necessary in every home today as it always has been. You flip on a switch and some magical fairy in your wall creates the miracle of light. Well, maybe that's not the way it really works, but good lighting, from wherever it comes, is essential to your home. And lovely and practical lamps are available that will blend into your decor — or stand out as unique, if that's what you prefer. You can find everything from old sconces meant for candles to oil lamps and hanging chandeliers. And heads up while you shop: Some of the best lighting buys you can find are right above you, hanging from the rafters, and often overlooked or forgotten. Don't forget to look for a price tag on a light that seems to be illuminating the booth or display in which it's sitting. It could be another of those overlooked gems that's actually for sale, too.

Freestanding Oil Lamps

Oil lamps have an aesthetic presence from the past, and they look lovely merely adorning a table as a knick-knack. Lamps that are in good shape, though, no matter how old, can have a practical purpose. They'll light your house on a dark, stormy night when the power has gone out, or when a soft, romantic flicker is the order of the occasion. But be careful when you buy oil lamps. Unless you're an expert, it's tough to tell the difference between old and new ones, and plenty of inexperienced shoppers have carted home fairly new oil lamps at antique lamp prices. Here are two ways to tell the difference:

Method 1. The best way to spot a lamp of recent years is to look at the collar — the round ring between the burner and the lamp base. Old lamps have collars that are cemented in place; new ones have collars that screw into place. If the oil lamp you're considering has a screw-on collar, much like a screw-on jar lid, it's a fairly new piece, made sometime well into the twentieth century. That doesn't mean you shouldn't buy it, though. If it's beautiful and fits into your decorating scheme, age shouldn't matter. Just don't pay a high price for a newer lamp. A dollar amount considerably under $50 will buy just about any oil lamp produced within the last thirty or forty years. An exception is Aladdin lamps, a particular brand of oil lamps that has seen continual popularity for years. Aladdin lamps, identified as such on the piece, retain a high resale value regardless of age.

Method 2. Many dealers, in their attempt to deceive, will buy a reproduction collar and cement it to the base of a newer oil lamp. Review the basics of recognizing old glass (see chapter 6), and apply the same standards to an oil lamp. If the lamp is old, there will definitely be signs of use, since all oil lamps were originally meant to be used. Look for fine scratches on the bottom or high and low spots on which the lamp has rested. If the lamp is metal, you can also look for signs of age and wear: gradual wearing away of plating in areas that have been handled, dings and dents, an even timeworn patina. Age shows, so grab your magnifying glass and look for it.

When you purchase an oil lamp, make sure the font contains no cracks. The burner should be in good shape, too, with a handle that turns freely. If there is no burner, most lighting stores carry new ones that will work with your lamp. If you intend to use your oil lamp — and good oil lamps, regardless of age, are quite usable — make sure you have a new wick. Many lamps already come with a wick, but old wicks are often brittle, saturated with

These oil lamps are tiny and were meant to be carried from room to room. Their parts are in good working order, and their fonts are filled with kerosene. All it takes to press them back into service is a match.

something that may or may not be oil, and some simply won't light properly because of their age. Inexpensive lamp wicking can be found in most lighting stores, too, and you'll often run across vintage lighting displays in antiques shows and malls that offer the oil lamp supplies you need.

One word of caution! Never, *never* use old oil that comes in your lamp. There is no telling what it really is; it might be not lamp oil at all but some other highly flammable substance. When they run out of oil, people have actually been known to use gasoline and other liquids that ignite. You don't want to be the one to strike a match to a font full of gasoline. Lamp oil, which is really kerosene, can be purchased in hardware and many department stores, and it's available in different colors and scents. Consider colorless oil, though, if you use the lamp frequently: The pretty color that matches your decor will also leach through the wick and discolor the lamp's metal collar, as well as the burner. Still, there's nothing lovelier than a clear-glass oil lamp with red or green oil in its font at Christmastime, or a font filled with blue oil for Hanukkah. Special colors for special occasions can be quite decorative and festive, but for regular use, switch back to colorless. Besides the obvious prevention of damage to the metal lamp parts, plain kerosene is considerably cheaper when bought in large quantities.

Oil Lamp Safety

Never leave an oil lamp unattended, and never light or place your burning oil lamp near curtains or drapes.

Converting an Oil Lamp

Yes, many people do buy oil lamps with the intention of converting them to electricity. In fact, you'll be amazed at all the items people convert into electric lamps. Buckets, fire extinguishers, dolls, canning jars full of buttons, tools; virtually anything can be turned into a

Using an Oil Lamp

1. Lighting an oil lamp is simple. After making sure the font is filled with lamp oil, remove the glass chimney.

2. Check the quality of the wick. If it's old and brittle, insert a fresh one. Turn the handle on the burner until about ½-inch (1.3 cm) of wick is exposed and light it.

3. Back the wick down at least halfway by turning the handle. Too much wick exposed will cause a fast burn and lots of black smoke.

4. Replace the chimney, being careful not to burn your fingers.

At first, you'll notice a definite smell coming from the burning oil. It's not pleasant, but it will dissipate within a few minutes. This means that if your guests will be arriving in half an hour, you should give the oil lamp a fifteen-minute head start so they won't have to experience the kerosene fumes.

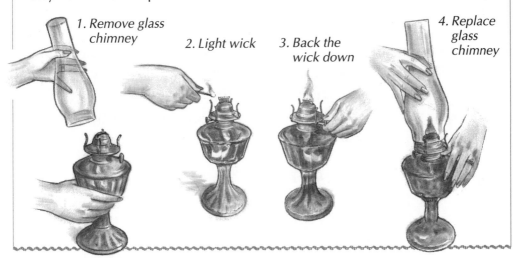

1. Remove glass chimney

2. Light wick

3. Back the wick down

4. Replace glass chimney

lamp of some sort. One antiques dealer found a pretty Tippecanoe bottle, drilled a hole through it for the lamp mechanism, and turned it into a nice little desk lamp. His asking price was $50. Not too bad, considering the bottle he used was over a hundred years old. Normally, the bottle — a common variety known to avid bottle collectors — was worth around $100. But in this case, the bottle was a rare color, driving the price up to around $500 for a

If this bottle were intended to be a lamp, it would have come fully equipped. Before converting any object to another use, be sure you know what you have. This rare bottle is worth far more intact than it would be as a lamp, no matter how seamless the conversion.

perfect specimen. His was in perfect shape before he drilled the hole, and when his big blunder was pointed out, he yanked all the light mechanisms off the bottle and put it back on the market as a bottle, asking the top book price for it. Unfortunately, the bottle still had that dreadful hole, and with or without the lamp attachments, it was worth only the $50 he'd originally asked.

The moral of this story is to find out the value of what you're about to turn into a lamp, or convert to electricity, if you intend to alter its structure in any manner, such as by drilling. When you make permanent changes, you can substantially decrease the item's book value — or create a piece that has no collectible or antique value at all. So be careful.

A better way to convert a lamp to electricity is to use a kit. Such kits, which can make the change without drilling or damaging the original lamp, are available in lighting stores and lighting booths at antiques shows and flea markets. When you make this conversion, you may just save a $500 bottle from a $50 death.

Floor and Table Lamps

Electric lamps became popular urban items during the early part of the twentieth century, but believe it or not, some rural communities in the United States did not receive electricity until the 1940s. Whenever electricity came to an area, though, oil lamps were immediately converted into electric as a practical alternative to buying all new lamps. In short, it was cheaper to adapt what you already had than to run out and buy new. Thus some of the earlier electric lamps you'll see are actually original conversions. And since these conversions were made with no intent to safeguard any antique value in the lamp, many collectible and expensive lamps were stripped of value. Consequently, when you begin to buy vintage lighting, note that the older electric lights specifically made for use with electricity will usually cost more than early conversions, and they will retain a better market value over the years. Still, many of the older converted pieces are beautiful, and while they aren't as collectible, they can still be a great addition to any room in your home. In fact, some of the best lighting bargains can be found in converted lamps. Just make sure you know what you're buying when you seek out electric lights, because many people have paid a high price for something that was converted and not realized what they were really getting. *No converted lamp should sell for as much as another like it in its original condition.*

When you start to think about buying an older lamp, there are a few guidelines to follow:

- **Make sure it sits level.** Rocking lamps are annoying, and they can be a real hazard if they tip easily. So, no matter what kind of lamp you choose — floor or table — a level lamp is best.
- **Check for a finial** — the decorative piece that screws into the top to hold a lamp shade in place. If you find an obvious screw hole at the top, but it's empty, the finial is missing. Unfortunately, it's rare to find an older lamp with its original finial these days, but if you do, the addition of that one little piece will increase the asking price. On the other hand, the lack of a finial should decrease the book value, so point out the empty screw hole to the dealer and ask for a little more off the price, since the lamp isn't intact. Then go to a hardware or lighting store and buy a brand-new replacement finial for $3 or $4.

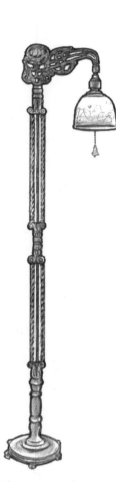

This is one of my favorite reading lamps. Dating from the early twentieth century, it's solid brass and cost — with vintage glass shade included — just $75. New pieces can't compare with that value and quality.

- **Take a good look at the wiring.** In most cases, original or old wiring should be replaced: It can become brittle and turn into a fire hazard. Check the cord, too. Old cord, like old wiring, should be replaced, but the good news is that if you really like the look of the old cloth-covered cords used sixty years ago, these are being reproduced and sold in many lighting stores.

- **Look at the way the cord is attached to the lamp.** In floor lamps, the cord will work one of two ways. It will either fit through a hollowed-out place in the post that connects the stand to the lighting fixture, thus concealing the cord, or it will merely wind up the post from the stand to the lighting fixture and be visible. Make sure you like the looks of the cord arrangement before you buy the lamp.

- **See what kind of lamp shade will be required.** Some lamps take traditional fabric shades; others — particularly those with arms that extend downward — require a glass one. If a glass shade is required, try a shade on the lamp before you make the purchase to be sure all the pieces that hold the shade into place are there. Also, when a lamp has an extended arm for its shade, make sure that this arm is secure and will remain where you put it instead of gradually slipping.

- **Check the mechanism by which you turn on the light** to make sure you like it and it works. It will either be a pull chain or a traditional turning knob. Pull chains can be converted into knobs and vice versa. Parts are available in lighting stores.

Shades

Currently, it's quite popular to purchase an old lamp and place a new cloth shade on it — one that resembles a shade made seventy or eighty years ago. Shades from that era are rare, and when they are found, their condition is usually pretty bad: frayed, yellowed, and brittle. But within the past several years, the art of making beautiful vintage-looking shades has become popular, and these look better on old lighting than most existing older shades. The cost for these shades was fairly high when they first hit the market but is now gradually decreasing. In this case, with the advantage of overall better condition and looks, a new shade could actually be preferable to an older one.

When you're buying a shade for any older lamp, take the lamp along with you if possible. Not all shades work with every lamp. Sometimes shade styles don't look good, sizes don't fit, or fabrics don't match. Whatever the case, if you intend to invest the money to buy an older lamp, go the extra mile when you purchase the shade and try it on the lamp first.

In the case of an older glass shade, the first thing to do is check for cracks. These normally originate at the top of the shade, where it attaches to the lamp. Hairline cracks just a fraction of an inch long are considered normal wear and usually won't get any longer, but if the crack is much more than a fourth of an inch long, don't buy the shade. These longer cracks often indicate a weakness in the glass. Also, some roughness around the top edge is common; don't let it worry you if the shade you love seems a little crude in craftsmanship. It was merely an old manufacturing technique seen particularly in the less expensive shades. Newer glass lamp shades, and older ones of high quality, have polished rims around the top; cracking should not be present.

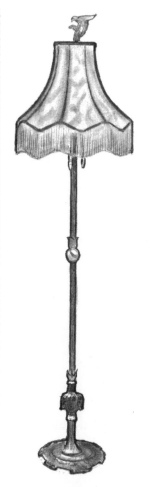

Another early twentieth century piece, this solid brass floor lamp came complete with its original finial and painted base. The shade is new, in keeping with the style of the original shade and made specifically for this lamp.

Hanging, Ceiling-Mounted, and Wall-Mounted Lamps

If you buy one of these lamps for functional use, make sure it's completely intact and in good working shape. Nice examples of hanging and wall-mounted oil lamps are available, but many people have made the purchase only to discover that some of the necessary pieces are missing once they try to install the lamp. In many cases, the missing pieces from older lamps are very difficult, if not impossible, to replace. Inspect the lamp carefully, manipulate all the working moving parts, light it up, and apply some common sense before you buy, or you could end up with something that will serve only as a knick-knack. Consider the following questions:

◆ If the lamp is to be mounted to the wall, does a wall bracket come with it? Does the bracket seem to be original to the lamp, or could it have been added later? Does it work with the lamp?
◆ Most wall-mounted oil lamps had either tin or mercury reflectors. Does the wall-mounted model you're considering have its reflector? Does the reflector attach securely?
◆ If the bracket, reflector, and lamp holder are intact, is there a font for the oil? Does it have a burner and chimney? Does the lamp fit securely in its holder, or does it jiggle around?

And in the case of a hanging oil lamp:

◆ Is there a decorative shade to cover the actual lamp? Any cracks or chips in it? Does it fit securely into its holder?
◆ Are the lamp font, burner, and chimney all there?

One simple oil lamp like this 1880 model can light up an entire room, especially if it comes equipped with its original reflector. Mercury vapor was used to create the silvering on this particular reflector.

- Are the chains with which to hang it from the ceiling intact?
- Is there a ceiling-mount bracket and a decorative cover plate?

Ask yourself similar questions if you are considering an electric ceiling or wall-mounted lamp. Is everything there, including the brackets you'll need for mounting the lamp? Nothing is more disappointing than buying the perfect lamp or lighting fixture and taking it home, only to discover part of it missing. If this does happen to you, most lighting and some hardware stores will sell the parts you need, and while having everything original is always better, in lighting it's often quite difficult. New parts may affect book value, but you might not have a choice if you'd like your vintage light to work. And again, check the wiring. Avoid using it if you can, and if you don't know how to rewire a lamp, look in the yellow pages for a lighting store. Someone there will be able to help you, or even do it for you. Also, antiques and collectibles dealers who specialize in vintage lighting will know how to do the rewiring.

KNICKKNACKS

This category, more than anything else you will buy, is open to personal preference. Virtually everything has the potential to become a knickknack, and when you start browsing the shops and malls, you'll find that certain things will strike your fancy. You may fall in love with a mounted swordfish, or maybe an old pitcher and wash basin set is just the thing you've been looking for.

Knickknacks can fill out a home and make it cozy and comfortable. They can be the icing on the cake, if you like knickknacks. Or they can be an annoyance, a distraction, and something you'll have to dust every few days, like it or not. Your preferences in knickknacks depend on your likes and dislikes, and if you're not sure what you really want yet, it's probably best to wait with the accessories until you've finished furnishing the room, or your entire house, and lived in it for a while. Then you can decide if you want to add a few finishing touches or forget them altogether.

If you decide to leave the room as it is, that's fine. The biggest advantage to skipping the knickknacks is avoiding maintenance, because everything you add to your living space comes with a certain amount of upkeep. If you do want to fill out the bare spots, however — put a few odds and ends on the wall, line a shelf with something pleasant and homey — here are a few popular items that can still be found at reasonable prices.

Just about anything looks great stashed in an old canning jar. Some of the more collectible varieties come with a hefty price tag, but common, everyday jars such as this are still available for a few dollars. Don't can in them, though — the new ones are better for that.

- ◆ **Bottles.** Nothing is prettier than a few of the great old cobalt blues lined up on a windowsill, catching the sun. Display old bottles according to the purpose of the room: food bottles for the kitchen, medicine bottles for the bathroom, wine bottles for the dining table, perfume bottles for the bedroom. And *never* put water in old bottles. Water contains lime and other minerals that will deposit on the glass and eventually destroy it. Antique glass bottles can be professionally cleaned, removing the lime deposits and any damage they've caused, but the process is both costly and time consuming. If your intent is to use an old bottle as a vase, then, buy a vase, or go to a home furnishings store and buy one of the lovely reproductions of an old bottle instead.

Cleaning Bottles

Ridding old bottles of cloudiness, flaking, or mineral deposits is best left to the professionals, and normally glass cleaners can be found within antique bottle circles. If you have a bottle that needs to be cleaned, ask any dealer who has a prominent display of old bottles how to go about it. Most likely she'll be able to lead you in the right direction. There are a few little tricks you can use, though, that might save you time and money:

- Never use any lime-cleaning agents, even if it looks like your bottle has a mineral buildup. *Household cleaning agents will destroy old glass by turning it milky or cloudy.*
- Grab a small handful of unpopped popcorn and drop it in the bottle. Add a little water and shake vigorously. You may have to repeat this several times to knock hardened particles loose.
- If the internal glass appears a little cloudy, coat the inside of the bottle lightly with cooking oil.

- **Vases.** Pottery and porcelain pieces are quite collectible, but often pricey. Good glass examples can still be found for only a few dollars.

- **Wooden planes, graniteware, milk cans, earthenware jugs, baskets, wooden crates, vintage toys, and anything else of moderate size** can make nice floor groupings. Even an old slop bucket (a bucket into which an old chamber pot or bedpan was emptied) can make a nice display in just the right spot, such as next to a washstand. There really is no limit to what you can set in an out-of-the-way place on your floor, but make sure it's off your beaten path, because an inadvertent kick or bump can cause untold

Flat, unmarked, hand-painted porcelain vases like these were popular in the late nineteenth century, selling for $1 or less, usually. Today they can be had for just a few dollars more than the original price.

Few things have more character than an old clock. This wall model dates to the mid-nineteenth century, and with some modest restoration has found new life telling time in the twenty-first century. Wall clocks, traditionally one of the most popular of all clock categories, were produced in hundreds of different styles during the nineteenth century.

damage. And if you have small children or pets, you may want to reconsider the wisdom of grouping on the floor anything that will dent or break.

- **Clocks.** Major money can be invested in an old timepiece, but less expensive clocks are always available, too. Before you buy, consider if you want the clock to serve as a piece of furniture (as a long-case clock would), of if you'd prefer something smaller, such as a wall or mantel clock. Always check to see if the clock works, and if you can, observe it for several hours before you buy it to make sure it keeps accurate time. Ask the dealer to open up the clock so you can examine the condition of the mechanism. Even an untrained eye can spot rust and other damage.

- **Books.** Yes, old books make wonderful knickknacks. Several volumes on a shelf look classy, and if you choose those volumes carefully, you might just have several months' worth of good reading material. And the best news about old books is that because they're plentiful, they're also very inexpensive.

- **Old prints, calendars, paintings, and framed magazine covers** look lovely hanging on the wall. Keep paintings and anything paper out of direct sunlight, however, even if covered by glass. Light will make paper fade. Also, add an old frame to something new while you're at it. Old frames are cheap, and they can turn something plain or ordinary into something fancy and eye catching.

- **Vintage fabrics, tapestries, and needlework** are also great decorations. They, too, should be kept out of direct sunlight to prevent fading. The popularity of fabric items — crewel embroidery, for example — is growing, and so are the prices, so when you make a purchase, take a careful look at what you're buying. Use a magnifying glass to spot moth or other insect damage. Look carefully for water or mildew spots. And if you're not an expert, *do not* invest a large amount of money based on a dealer's word that the quilt or cross-stitch sampler is old. New techniques can replicate old ones quite easily, and many brand-new imported handmade pieces are being sold as vintage or antique. Get a guarantee that what you're buying is what it's represented to be, or find an expert who will advise you, before you open your bank vault. *Old quilts and samplers can be wonderful investment-quality collectibles, but you must know what you're investing in before you make the final deal.*

- **Doilies** are a nice touch. Traditionally, they were placed on the backs of couches and chairs to prevent hair from coming into contact with the fabric. They were also placed under knickknacks to prevent scratching. Old handmade doilies are inexpensive and quite abundant.

- **Candlestick holders.** Glass, pottery, and brass candlestick holders are both decorative and practical. One word of caution, however: Candlestick holders usually come in pairs, and the best market and resale value is seen only in the ones that are still in pairs. Singles will bring significantly less than half the value of a pair, if you intend to sell your candlestick holders someday. Of course, since singles sell for much less than a pair, if you're not interested in an immediate resale potential finding that exact match can give you hours, months, or even several years' worth of excuses to go hunting.

Nothing makes a room cozier than a homespun needlepoint sampler. This piece is a family heirloom that is sure to adorn the walls of future generations.

I Bought It but Now I Don't Like It

Or maybe you've lived with it for a while and discovered it's not what you wanted, needed, or hoped for, or it just doesn't fit in with the rest of your home. This happens all the time. You become enamored with it on discovery, then disillusioned later on. If it's a $5 trinket, there's not much of a problem. Give it to someone who will appreciate it, or stick it in your closet, up on the top shelf, way back in the darkest corner, and forget about it for ten or fifteen years. Something more expensive, though, won't be quite so easy to deal with when you decide it's not the piece for you.

You do have a few options for ridding yourself of the Victorian table that cost a fortune but doesn't fit into the setting for which it was intended.

Give it away as a gift. Granted, you've paid several hundred dollars for it, but when you weigh all the factors involved, money may not turn out to be the primary consideration. Getting rid of the table is, because it's in the way, or it looks so bad in its place it detracts from everything else you've done to make your home beautiful, or you can't stand the sight of it anymore. So maybe you have a friend or loved one who has admired that treasure-turned-eyesore every time he has entered your home and would truly appreciate it as a gift. If that's the case, and you can afford such an extravagance, put a big red bow on the table and give it to him. And don't turn out to be one of those people who will give something away under the condition that if you ever change your mind, or the furnishings in your home, you'll want it back. Part with that table for good, knowing that something you loved for a few exciting moments is going to a far better place.

Advertise it in your local newspaper. Be accurate in the description (see page 208 for a list of accepted

Though something as simple as an old honey bucket, or slop jar, can add visual interest to any room, if your mind can't get past its original function, give it away.

quality descriptions). Advertise the price, too, in order to separate the real antiques seekers who are willing to pay the price from those who are merely looking for a bargain. Just make sure you ask enough to cover your initial investment in the table plus a little extra pocket money. Also add a cushion of 10 to 15 percent above what you want to realize from the deal so you can discount it by that much and let the buyer think she has made a real deal.

Sell it to a dealer directly, as you learned in chapter 5. Make the rounds of the malls, shows, and stores with the things you want to unload, using the above pricing formula.

You can also keep the table, place it in storage, or try it in another room than that for which it was intended, with the idea that since you did fall in love with it once, there must still be something redeemable in it. Maybe you can just throw a tablecloth over it and leave it where it is, or stick it in the guest room. Try putting it in the entry hall covered with framed family photos. Use it in a bedroom for a lamp table, or stash it in a home office and stack books on it. Whatever you choose to do, give yourself some time before you act, because when you get rid of it, you could regret your decision later. In other words, give your first impression a chance. Somewhere down the line you might just fall in love with that table all over again.

This c. 1880 print, in its original frame, was a bargain at $60. Though it's widely reproduced today, this original print came from Germany.

Buying a Gift

Just about anything you'd purchase for your own home is appropriate to give as a gift. Make sure the recipient is someone who will appreciate vintage merchandise for what it is, however, and who won't think of it as merely something used. Face it — not all people have a true appreciation for antiques and collectibles. There are actually some people out there who would choose new over vintage any time, and as hard as it is to believe, some of those people might just be your friends.

Once you've established that your gift recipient has all the wonderful qualities it takes to appreciate a vintage gift — vision, imagination, practicality, love of the old — the next thing to do is decide if the gift will be a personal one or something more practical.

- **Bridal shower and wedding gifts** are usually practical. Consider buying a whole array of kitchen utensils or some vintage cookbooks as a bridal shower gift, or an entire set of peanut butter glasses or china for a wedding. Vintage linens and doilies make wonderful wedding gifts, too. And if you can find one in good shape, an old photo album or frame for a wedding picture makes a lovely present. Or maybe luggage would fit the occasion — something old, something stylish, or something very 1960s.

They're ugly. They're bright. They've got flowers that will make your eyes water. And they're definitely from the 1960s. Where else but in an antiques mall can you find such treasures?

- **Birthday gifts** should definitely be personal. Birthdays give you the chance to match a person's preferences to any number of odds and ends. Books, old pocketwatches, ink pens, jewelry, vintage clothing, cuff links, favorite childhood toys . . . the sky is the limit. If you look hard enough, maybe you'll stumble across an old Schwinn bike like the one he used when he was a kid and has talked about for the past twenty years, or a sled or Daisy air rifle. Items associated with a profession are always good personal choices, too. An old medical kit is great for a physician, tools work for a carpenter, law books for a lawyer, old ledgers for the accountant, pens and pencils for a writer; again, you're limited only by your imagination. And if you can't match a profession, try a hobby. Fishing poles and other equipment are plentiful for the angler, cameras and photography supplies are available for the shutterbug, and sheet music can be found almost anywhere for the musician.

♦ **Holiday gifts** can be either practical or personal. Christmas and Hanukkah presents are up for grabs, but it's almost a sure bet that anything you give for Valentine's Day or an anniversary had better be personal.

Whatever you choose, no matter if it's practical or personal, keep the interests and lifestyle of the recipient in mind when you make a selection. You're buying a gift that can't be returned.

BUYING AND BUYING AND BUYING

It's easy to make buying itself the goal of antiques and collectibles shopping. You go to the antiques mall and you absolutely have to buy something before you go home. As your hunt continues and you haven't found just that right item to take home, you are pressed with the urgency that you've got to get it — whatever it is — before you reach the EXIT sign. Your heart starts pounding a little harder as you see that sign looming in the distance and realize your hands are still empty. And your breathing accelerates as the yards to the parking lot are shortening and you still haven't found it. One hundred yards, eighty yards, sixty yards, and nothing. Fifty yards, forty, thirty . . .

The countdown is almost complete and you're breaking into a cold sweat because you still haven't found anything to buy. Your hands are starting to shake, you're getting a little dizzy, then suddenly — there it is, right in front of your eyes. A moth-eaten, taxidermied beaver, his front teeth chipped and his broken tail covered with cobwebs, is calling your name. No one else is looking at it, thank heavens, so you quicken your pace until you reach it, then snatch it up into your arms and heave a big sigh of relief. It's yours. Your heart rate is returning to normal, and your breathing is evening out. The cold sweat has disappeared. The mighty shopper has at long last made a score.

This may seem like an extreme example, but buying can become an obsession, and if you're the one who really has to have that old beaver, you are obsessed. Admit it. If you can't, ask yourself several important questions. The answers will be pretty revealing.

- **How often do you walk away empty handed?** If you answer "never," that's a good indication that your shopping is controlling you instead of the other way around.
- **How often do you buy something you later regret?** If you answer "often," it probably means you aren't cautious in your purchases; you're buying for the sake of buying, not collecting or furnishing your home. In other words, you buy first, then think about what you've bought afterward. Try doing it the other way around.
- **How often do you spend much more than you originally intended?** If you answer "frequently," it's time to reevaluate your spending habits, because they're not completely under control. Think about your children's lunch money as you plunk down that cash.

- **How often do you spend money you can't afford or don't have?** If you answer "all the time," it's time to stay out of antiques and collectibles venues. You've climbed to the top of the obsession pole and are balancing pretty precariously up there.

People do become obsessed with antiques and collectibles, and anyone caught up in the lifestyle knows what the obsession is like from personal experience, or has witnessed it firsthand. It's an easy obsession to satiate since antiques and collectibles are sold everywhere, but it can be very damaging financially, not to mention emotionally. And once you've discovered real treasure, human nature lures you back to look for more.

The French philosopher Blaise Pascal once said, "Too much noise deafens us; too much light blinds us; too great a distance or too much of proximity equally prevents us from being able to see." Too much of an obsession can ruin our love for the antiques and collectibles that make our lives comfortable. When you see the symptoms in yourself, step back and take a breather. Get away from the buying and browsing for a while. Indulge in a few good books on antiques and study them if you really need an antiques fix in your life, but refrain from buying *anything* until the dogged urge to buy is replaced with the joy you felt when you were a beginner, shopping for things to make your home more comfortable. Stay away from the traveling flea market that comes to town every other month. Avoid driving anywhere near an antiques mall, and don't log on to your favorite on-line antiques site — not even if you're breaking into a cold sweat and your hands are trembling. If you do, you'll eventually ruin your true passion for antiques.

Old books are some of the most underrated collectibles because they are so plentiful. If you'd like to learn how common English grammar has changed over the years, satisfy your curiosity and buy a classic primer.

When at last you return to your regular shopping outlets, proceed slowly. Leave the credit cards and checkbook at home. Carry only a small amount of cash. Spend only an hour or two browsing, and think of it as a treat, not something you absolutely have to do.

Early twentieth century hymn books like these are easily found and contain some of my church choir's favorite Sunday anthems. They also can inspire joy, reverence, and frugality.

AND FINALLY . . .

Volumes have been written on how to buy antiques and what to do with them once you own them. If you find you've amassed more than you can manage, you can learn how to become an antiques dealer, or you can learn how to do simple restorations. Whatever you need to know about any antique or collectible is recorded in print somewhere, and most of the volumes you will read will offer different advice. It's strictly up to you which suggestions to heed and which to discard — and that applies to this book, too. However, there are two things you must remember as you close the pages of this volume:

Tip #1. There are no decorating rules for your everyday antiques. What you buy, and how you use it, is purely a matter of choice. Don't let anyone tell you otherwise.

Tip #2. Hands-on experience is what will eventually offer you the greatest knowledge. Book learning definitely helps, but in order to know if your glass lamp is authentically old or the patina on a brass candlestick is real, you must first examine hundreds of glass lamps or brass candlesticks. There is no substitute for a hands-on education.

Epilogue

or too many years, the popular image of an antiques collector was someone with her nose pointed straight in the air who wouldn't bat an eye at plunking down $10,000 for an old vase. I've never plunked down $10,000 for any antique, and I probably never will. Why? The answer is simple. Everyday antiques are for everyday people now. There's no more mystique surrounding them. All of us can participate, whether we have $10 in our pockets or $10,000. What was once a veritable no-man's-land has finally divested itself of its snooty aura and taken on a friendlier look. Everyone with a true appreciation for the old has a chance to partake. Sure, when you begin to invest in the finest-class antiques you'll find yourself in that same no-man's-land where very few can indulge. But overall, the world of antiques is moving in the direction of people like me, who get excited when they find a great old ice cream scoop. And the numbers and varieties of people who are discovering antiques and collectibles are truly amazing. Quite honestly, in most antiques circles these days there *is* no stereotypical buyer.

And as I've stated several times in the pages of this book, there are no rules about what you can and can't collect, nor are there rules about the things you choose for your home. We don't have dictates of good decorating etiquette weighing us down anymore. We can do whatever we like, whenever we like.

So do it your way. Buy whatever you fall in love with, use it in any way it fits into your home or life. And last but not least — have fun as you hunt and shop. There has never been a better time to find the everyday antiques and collectibles that will make your life better. They're out there waiting for you. Happy hunting!

Helpful Resources

Price and Identification Guides

Husfloen, Kyle, ed. *Antiques & Collectibles Price Guide: Antique Trader Books.* Dubuque, Iowa: Antique Trader, annual.

Huxford, Sharon, and Bob Huxford, eds. *Schroeder's Antiques Price Guide.* Paducah, KY: Collector Books, annual.

Kovel, Ralph M., and Terry H. Kovel. *Kovels' Antiques & Collectibles Price List.* New York: Crown Publishers Group, annual.

Maloney, David J. *Maloney's Antiques & Collectibles Resource Directory.* Dubuque, IA: Antique Trader, annual.

Miller, Judith, and Elizabeth Norfolk, eds. *Miller's International Antiques Price Guide.* Suffolk, England: Antique Collectors' Club, annual.

Rinker, Harry L. *Harry L. Rinker Official Price Guide to Collectibles.* New York: Ballantine Books, Inc., annual.

———. *The Official Price Guide to Antiques and Collectibles.* New York: Ballantine Books, Inc., annual.

———. *The Official Price Guide to Flea Market Treasures.* New York: Ballantine Books, Inc., annual.

Schroy, Ellen, ed. *Warman's Antiques and Collectibles Price Guide.* Iola, WI: Krause Publications, annual.

Periodicals

Antique Trader Weekly, P.O. Box 1050, Dubuque, IA 52004-1050.

AntiqueWeek, P.O. Box 90, Knightstown, IN 46148. This publisher also compiles several regional guides to antiques shops, shows, and malls.

Collectors News & The Antique Reporter, P.O. Box 156, Grundy Center, IA 50638-0156.

Kovels on Antiques and Collectibles, Circulation Department, Kovels Publications, P.O. Box 1050, Dubuque, IA 52004-1050.

Warman's Today's Collector, Krause Publications, Inc., 700 East State Street, Iola, WI 54990.

Web Sites

Antiques Sales
www.collectoronline.com
www.antiquesonline.com
www.antiquingonline.com
www.collect.com
www.antiquesworld.com
www.antiqueclub.com
www.rubylane.com
www.collectiblesnet.com
www.elegantantiques.com
www.heartland-discoveries.com
www.antiquepeddlersmall.com
www.shoplocator.com

Auctions On-Line
www.ebay.com
www.goldnage.com
www.liveauctiononline.com
www.auctions.amazon.com
www.ehammer.com
www.auctionuniverse.com
www.boxlot.com
www.dapllc.com *(for lamp lovers only)*
www.potteryauction.com
www.buffalobid.com
www.utrade.com

www.auctionworks.com
www.auctions.yahoo.com
www.utome.com
www.tias.com
www.tace.com
www.quiltcollector.com

General Information
www.kovel.com
www.krause.com/collectibles/tc
www.rinker.com

Glossary

Absentee bid: A bid left with an auctioneer by someone who isn't attending the auction.

Art pottery: Decorative ceramic objects that have artistic rather than utilitarian uses.

Auction house: A place at which auctions are held on a regular basis.

Antiqued: Not antique, but altered or produced to look old.

Art Deco: Collectibles dating from 1920 to 1940 that are marked by straight, clean, modern lines. Particularly popular in furniture and architecture.

Art Nouveau: Collectibles dating from 1880 to 1914, influenced by the French style, and usually marked by swirls and flowing sequences such as floral scenes and women with long hair; popular in jewelry and glass decorations.

Arts & Crafts: A late-nineteenth- and early-twentieth-century movement of back-to-basics craftsmanship and style. It was a reaction to industrialization.

Bakelite: A synthetic resin patented in 1907 that became popular in American jewelry manufacturing during the 1930s. *Highly collectible!*

Ball-and-claw feet: Used on furniture; talons or claws grasping a ball. The ball is most often glass.

Barter: In deal making, the exchange of goods or labor for other goods or labor without the exchange of money.

Bone china: Porcelain made of 25 percent china clay, 25 percent china stone, and 50 percent ground cattle bone. Became popular in the early nineteenth century.

Book value: Value as stated in the pricing guides.

Breakfront: A piece of furniture, typically a bookcase or cabinet, where the straight plane of the front is interrupted, or broken; the middle section protrudes slightly beyond the side sections.

Bun feet: Flattened ball feet on furniture; common in the late seventeenth century.

Cabriole leg: An elongated furniture leg in the shape of an S, often with a pronounced knee; popular in the Queen Anne style.

China: A fine porcelain made of clay and specially baked; originally imported from China.

Chippendale: Furniture marked by substantial finely carved ornamentation and the free use of curves. It is sturdy and characterized by ball-and-claw feet.

Colonial style: The term used to describe furniture dating to the period when America was still one of the British colonies, 1625–1776.

Commode: In seventeenth-century France, a low chest of drawers; in America, a bedroom cupboard with a portable latrine.

Consignment sale: An auction where the sellers pay a commission to have their items sold.

Crazing: A defect in ceramics that causes fine lines to appear.

Crewel work: Embroidery in wool threads on white or beige linen.

Delftware: Earthenware first made in Delft, Holland, in the late sixteenth century. It was later made in England, too.

Dovetail: A furniture production technique: Two sections, such as drawer sides, are held together by a projecting tenon fitting into a matching cutout known as a mortise, much the way two pieces of a puzzle fit together. In early furniture, this is a mark of a handmade piece.

Duncan Phyfe: Furniture maker who copied popular furniture styles and trends from 1800 to 1820; his work falls within the federal period.

Earthenware: Made of baked clay.

Ebonize: Blackening a cheap wood to make it look like ebony.

Electroplate: To cover items made of base metal such as brass with a thin layer of silver.

Enamel: Powdered glass mixed with flux (an alkaline product that contributes to the fusion of ingredients in glass) and a metallic oxide (a product that adds color). Enamels were and still are used to decorate metal.

Engraving: Cutting into a glass or metal object to inscribe a decoration.

Épergne: An ornamental dish with several compartments for fruits and other after-dinner sweets used as a centerpiece for a dining table.

Ephemera: Paper collectibles.

Étagére: Originally a connected set of display shelves mounted to the wall. Eventually it became a freestanding piece of furniture. Also known as a whatnot.

Faux: False.

Federal style: The term used to describe furniture made after the American Revolution, 1776–1830.

Flashed glass: A thin layer of colorful glass applied to another piece of glass.

Flatback: Pottery objects made to be viewed from the front only. The backs were left flat and unpainted.

Flatware: In silver, cutlery. In ceramics, flat dishes such as plate and saucers.

Flea market: A gathering of antiques and collectibles dealers in one location.

Fluting: A decoration consisting of long, rounded grooves.

Fretwork: Decorative carving or openwork, usually of interlacing lines.

Glaze: An opaque color. Also, in ceramics, a kiln-fired finish.

Gothic: An architectural style marked by arches, originally seen in the eleventh through the fifteenth centuries, then revived from 1750 to 1780 and again from 1800 to 1875.

Graining: Simulating a wood grain.

Hallmark: The identification stamps marked on gold or silver to indicate its standard of purity.

Highboy: One chest of drawers on top of another; it was popular starting in the late seventeenth century. Also known as a tallboy.

House number: The number assigned to the auctioneer so he can make his own bids.

Iridescent glass: Glass colored to make it look like a rainbow; it was popular in the late nineteenth century.

Ironstone: A hard, white stoneware made by adding any of the various hard iron ores.

Jardinière: An ornamental bowl, pot, or stand for flowers or plants.

Lithography: The method of printing from a flat stone or metal plate.

Long-case clock: A tall, narrow clock with a base that sits on the floor. Also known as a tall-case clock or grandfather clock.

Lowboy: An eighteenth-century American dressing table or low chest of drawers made to match a highboy.

Lusterware: Highly glazed earthenware decorated by the application of metallic oxides into the glaze.

Majolica: Pottery produced in the United States and England during the nineteenth century that is enameled, glazed, richly colored, and decorated. It's not to be confused with Maiolica, a thirteenth-century Italian earthenware.

Mall: A large building where space is rented to several antiques and collectibles dealers for the purpose of selling their goods.

Orphans: Individual pieces once belonging to a set that are selling as single or separate units.

Patina: A thin coating or color change that results from age. Good, original patina enhances value. Destroying it decreases value.

Picker: Someone who shops for an antiques or collectibles dealer.

Porcelain: A fine, white, translucent, hard earthenware with a transparent glaze; china.

Polychrome: Describes something painted in several different colors.

Pontil: On the bottom of a glass object, a jagged, sharp knot or scar indicating that the piece was hand-blown.

Preview: Time allotted before an auction in which to examine merchandise.

Prints: Lithographs or other printed artwork that aren't hand-painted or drawn.

Provenance: An object's history. Verifiable provenance enhances value.

Reserve: The minimum price for which an item can be sold at auction.

Rococo: A decorative French style, 1720–1760, characterized by elaborate, detailed, and profuse ornamentation in the forms of scrolls, foliage, and shells.

Sampler: Fabric embroidered with various stitches and designs that traditionally demonstrated a young girl's skill in sewing.

Sconce: A candleholder made to hang on the wall.

Scout: Like a picker, someone who shops for a dealer, but in this case shops only for books.

Shard: A broken piece of pottery or glass.

Silvering: The reflective silver coating on the back of a mirror.

Slag glass: Swirled, multicolored glass used often as a lamp base and ornamentation.

Slip: Liquid clay used to decorate pottery, which is then known as slipware.

Slip seat: Removable seat of a wooden chair.

Smalls: Any small, collectible objects.

Sterling silver: In its pure state, silver is too soft to work with, so it is alloyed — usually with copper — to make it workable. Objects made from sterling are 925 out of 1,000 parts pure. In other words, they're 925 parts silver and 75 parts alloy.

Stoneware: A hard, nonporous pottery made from clay and feldspar; often resembles porcelain.

Usage mark: Any signs of wear that indicates an item has been used.

Veneer: Thin sheets of real wood glued to form a thicker and sturdier board.

Victorian: The period of antiques marked by the reign of Queen Victoria of England, 1837–1901.

Vintage: Something made in an earlier time.

Vitrine: A glass-front cabinet used for displaying fine pieces such as silver or china.

Washstand: A table holding a bowl and pitcher for washing the face and hands.

Glossary of Condition Terminology

Following are the standard classifications for the condition of an object, with one (1) being the very worst, and ten (10) the very best.

Parts, parts unit, or bad condition (1): Is not complete. Can be used for parts.

Worn (2): Bad shape. Largely intact, but is in a condition that will probably require major repair or restoration.

Fair (3): Condition is not great. May already have significant repair or alteration to the original. May have some obvious damage.

Average (4): Not good, not bad. Has value as a collectible and probably has good display potential. Probably does not have high resale value.

Very good (5): In overall good condition. Probably shows use and wear, but displays nicely and is not damaged.

Nice (6): In overall good condition, with the exception of a minor flaw (usually occurring in production) or discoloration. Good display quality.

Choice or excellent (7): Highly desirable piece. Great condition, other than the fact it has been used. Usually hold a high resale value.

New in box (8): Shows usage and age, but in great condition and still in its original container.

Mint (9): Almost as if it were new. Exceptional. Flawless. This piece is perfect and its value could be higher than what's listed in a price guide.

Mint in box (10): The most desirable and collectible condition. Exceptional. Flawless. Shows no wear. A perfect piece in its original container, possibly with original packing and instructions. This item will normally exceed the value listed in price guides.

Index

Note: Page numbers in *italics* indicate illustrations and photographs.

OTHER STOREY TITLES YOU WILL ENJOY

Antiques on the Cheap, by James W. McKenzie. Get the inside scoop on every aspect of antiquing— buying, cleaning, repairing, embellishing, refinishing, restoring, and selling. Expert advice for getting great deals at auctions, flea markets, and shops, and how to spot items that can be repaired to increase their value. Advice for selling antiques at flea markets, on consignment, and in shops is included. 224 pages. Paperback. ISBN 1-58017-073-0.

Be Your Own Home Decorator: Creating the Look You Love Without Spending a Fortune, by Pauline Guntlow. This inspiring guide proves that it doesn't have to be difficult or expensive to decorate with charm and taste. Presented with an infectious can-do attitude and clear step-by-step instructions, Guntlow explains how to customize kitchens, bedrooms, living rooms, and baths, and offers ways to maximize storage space. Whether a home needs a massive overhaul or a "quick-fix" solution to problem areas, this book provides dozens of unique possibilities. 144 pages. Paperback. ISBN 0-88266-945-1.

Buying & Selling Antiques: A Dealer's Inside View, by Sara Pitzer & Don Cline. A professional guide to getting started with minimal investment, identifying antiques that retain their value, even advice on auctions and auctioneers. 112 pages. Paperback. ISBN 0-88266-406-9.

The Rummager's Handbook: Finding, Buying, Cleaning, Fixing, Using, & Selling Secondhand Treasures, by R. S. McClurg. Antiquing as a fun and potentially profitable pastime has never been more popular, and this book offers hundreds of tips and ideas for finding sales and auctions, bargaining, determining value, and taking it home. 160 pages. Paperback. ISBN 0-88266-894-3.

Welcome Home: Tips for Creating a Haven for Mind, Body, and Spirit, by Elizabeth Knight. In response to the frantic pace of modern life, these simple tips and inspiring ideas will help readers create a warm, peaceful, and welcoming home environment. Packed with clever room-by-room suggestions for readers on making any place (even a hotel room) truly their own. Knight includes fascinating modern-day and age-old traditions from cultures around the world — the customs that transform a house into a home. 160 pages. Paperback. ISBN 1-58017-187-7.

These books and other Storey books are available at your bookstore, farm store, garden center, or directly from Storey Books, Schoolhouse Road, Pownal, Vermont 05261, or by calling 1-800-441-5700. Or visit our Web site at www.storeybooks.com